A Maine Hamlet

A *Maine Hamlet*

By LURA BEAM

Introduction by JERE DANIELL

The Maine Humanities Council *and*
the Maine Historical Society
with TILBURY HOUSE, *Publishers*

TILBURY HOUSE, *Publishers*
2 Mechanic Street
Gardiner, ME 04345
800-582-1899

MAINE HUMANITIES COUNCIL	MAINE HISTORICAL SOCIETY
P. O. Box 7202	485 Congress Street
Portland, ME 04112	Portland, ME 04101
207-773-5051	207-774-1822

Cover illustration: Lura Beam's grandparents pose in front of their Marshfield, Maine, home in this 1870s view. Photograph courtesy of Eileen Hayes. The house is no longer standing. (The image has been reversed.)

Cover design by Edith Allard; Introduction design by The Ascensius Press.

This reprint edition of A Maine Hamlet *was produced in conjunction with*
"The Mirror of Maine: The Maine Community in Myth and Reality,"
a library reading program sponsored by the Baxter Society and
funded by the Maine Humanities Council and the Rines-
Thompson Fund of the Maine Community Foundation.
It celebrates the publication of The Mirror of Maine,
an annotated bibliography of Maine books,
published in 2000 by the University of Maine Press
and the Baxter Society in collaboration with the Maine Historical Society.

Introduction

A Maine Hamlet describes the village folkways of Marshfield, Maine, in the decade 1894–1904. Lura Beam—who was born in 1887, lived with her grandparents in the community twelve years, spent summers there another five, and visited off and on thereafter—wrote the book a half century later in the 1950s. Friendship dictated her decision to write. Louise Bryant, with whom Beam shared a house in Bronxville, New York, had vacationed in and become intrigued with Marshfield. Bryant urged her companion to write about the community, and Beam obliged when it became clear her best friend would die soon. Life experience gave her the skill and confidence to complete the project. A graduate of Barnard with a master's degree from Columbia, Beam had been employed by several national organizations including the American Missionary Association and the American Association of University Women, had written two books as well as numerous articles and pamphlets, and was part of an intellectual circle which provided encouragement to any member with literary ambitions. Her own extraordinary memory, familiarity with both fiction set in rural communities and academic studies about them, sensitivity to how individuals and groups function, and ear for language all made the completed manuscript a gem. She had no difficulty finding a publisher.

My introduction to *A Maine Hamlet* came early. Soon after publication in 1957 my mother, who grew up in Machias less than two miles from where Beam's grandparents lived, obtained a copy which she proudly displayed in the living room of our Millinocket home. I was about to enter graduate

school in American Studies and remember reading the copy
with both personal and academic interest. A quarter century
later I reread *A Maine Hamlet* while testing the idea of com-
mitting myself to a long-term research project on the history
of New England towns. By then I was mature enough to
appreciate what Lura Beam had accomplished and began rec-
ommending the volume to most anyone who shared my growing fascination with the history of rural New England.
Republication of *A Maine Hamlet* by Lance Tapley in 1986
increased the volume's availability. Soon thereafter I made it
assigned reading on a bus tour which I guided from Eastport
to Bangor. We stopped in Marshfield (much to the astonish-
ment of residents who happened to be around), and were
greeted warmly by someone who had a key to the church and
opened it. I gave an impromptu mini-lecture, during the
course of which I had to confess how little I knew about either
Lura Beam or Marshfield. Were I giving that talk now I'd have
much more to say.

The Place

The Marshfield about which Beam wrote satisfied both
Webster's definition of a hamlet—"a cluster of houses in the
country"—and the sociological definition used in population
studies which labeled any location with less than 250 inhabitants a hamlet. Marshfield residents, however, rarely, if ever,
thought of their community in these terms. Marshfield was an
incorporated town with all the rights and responsibilities of
towns with much larger populations. It organized and
financed a school system, built and maintained roads, held
regular town meetings, and was proud of its political independence from the adjacent towns of Machias, East Machias,

Marshfield and surrounding towns. From Colby & Company, *Atlas of Washington County, Maine* (Houlton, Maine, 1881). Collection of the Maine Historical Society.

Northfield, and Whitneyville. I suspect Beam used the word "hamlet" instead of "town" in part because of the Shakespearean connotations. There's an edge of tragedy in the history of the people who lived in her hamlet. Beam, even in her formal academic publications, exhibited fondness for literary allusion.

Readers can get a good sense of Beam's Marshfield by looking at George Colby's 1881 *Atlas of Washington County.* The atlas (see maps) identifies individual home sites. Lura's mother was a Berry and the grandparents who raised Lura lived near the southeast corner of the town. No Beam homestead appears on the map, which suggests her father, who did serve as tax collector, bought property after 1881. The overall details of the map fit nicely with the descriptions in *A Maine Hamlet.* All but a few farmhouses were located near the east-west road along the town's southern border, and the triangle where the church sat.

Beam found Marshfield significantly changed when she returned in the early 1950s to gather information for her study. The change wasn't in population size or in the physical positioning of houses, but in the hamlet's relationship to Machias and East Machias, what together she calls the "town." Town and hamlet she saw having become more integrated, with the hamlet taking on more and more suburban characteristics. Constant out-migration had reduced the number of old families in Marshfield. The automobile allowed parents to work anywhere in the region. Communal institutions seemed less vital. Many of the friends she remembered had died.

My wife Elena and I visited Marshfield last month. More had changed between Beam's childhood and the fifties than since then. Although the population has doubled to about 450, most new house construction has been on what Beam

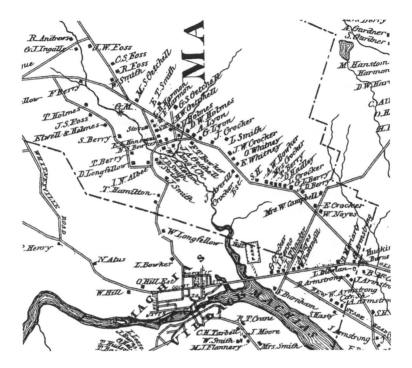

Southern half of Marshfield with property owners identified along
the principal east-west road. From Colby's 1881 *Atlas of Washington
County, Maine*. Collection of the Maine Historical Society.

called "the edge of town," especially on the roads to the Machiases. The location of dwellings along the east-west road seems much like that depicted in the old Colby atlas, although the houses themselves are different. The church rests, freshly painted, on the same site. One eighth-generation native to whom we talked says the suburbanization process continues. Marshfield has no schools of its own—even elementary students go to Machias—and no town hall. Its only community buildings are a fire station and the church. We asked about the farmhouse where Lura Beam's grandparents had lived. He said it had been torn down. Elena and I closed our visit by exploring the small burial ground close to where the farm had been. There we found several Berry headstones, but none for members of the Beam family.

The Author

Beam graduated from high school in 1904. Shortly thereafter her parents moved to a suburb of New York City. An accomplished student, who was also adventuresome, she enrolled at the University of California in Berkeley. Two years later she transferred to Barnard, the college for women at Columbia University, where she graduated in 1908. Then, making a bold commitment few women of her background considered, Beam moved south to teach black children in schools run by the American Missionary Association (AMA). She taught three years, served as an AMA administrator another six, then left the organization to work first for the Interchurch World Movement and soon thereafter the Association of American Colleges. Beam's visibility in the professional world took a huge leap forward with the publication of two co-authored books *A Thousand Marriages* (1931) and the *Single Woman*

(1934)—she and Dr. Robert Dickinson wrote for the National Committee on Maternal Health, which had hired her in 1927. The *Who's Who in America* recognized her accomplishments by including a biographical sketch in its 1936/1937 edition. Relatives and friends back in Marshfield probably knew of the honor and noted what a gifted child she had been. She was now fifty years old.

Beam's professional career peaked with the maternal health project. When its funds ran out she worked for short periods for several national organizations based in Washington, D.C., where she maintained an office. One was the American Association of University Women which published several educational pamphlets she wrote. The depression and World War II made full time jobs for academically oriented women scarce. When *Who's Who* started its regional publications in 1943, Beam was downgraded to *Who's Who in the East*. She disappeared from that listing after its first edition.

Meanwhile, changes in Beam's personal life had lessened her dependence on regular jobs as a source of income. While working on the maternal health project she developed a close relationship with its executive secretary, Louise Bryant. The women joined forces in what used to be called a "Boston marriage." Beam moved to Bryant's home in Bronxville: the two remained devoted companions until Bryant's death in 1957. Friendship, a home, and shared expenses freed Beam to pursue new interests. In that last *Who's Who* biography she listed "writer" among her occupational commitments and "appraisal of individual . . . and community" among her special interests. It's not difficult to imagine the circle of friends who gathered in Bronxville discussing the increasingly popular works on primitive communities written by fellow Barnard graduates Ruth Benedict, who was the same age as Beam, and Margaret Mead. At some point the Marshfield native began toying with the idea of doing a community study herself. But not of a primitive community off somewhere in the Pacific. One of her old mentors down south, Harlan Douglass, had published a book entitled *The Little Town* (1919) and urged Beam to write about the little town she knew so well. Douglass was dead, but not forgotten.

Beam's housemate provided the final stimulus. In the early 1950s, and perhaps earlier, the couple vacationed in the Machias area. Bryant could hardly contain her enthusiasm for what she saw in Marshfield. The foreword to *A Maine Hamlet* includes a brief comment on what happened afterwards. Beam added details to the story in the biography of her friend that she wrote later. After describing the now-published Marshfield study as "a memorial" of Bryant's "last holiday in Maine," Beam wrote: "this book dealt with a life so familiar to me that it needed no telling. But my urban companion was dazzled with the meaning of the United States in a place where the returning native could look at any house and tell its story back to the Civil War. She never stopped coaxing me to write down how it used to be." Lura had noted earlier that she hired her companion to copy manuscripts and that as Bryant's health had begun to decline rapidly, the copying seemed to help her spirits. The passage in the biography concluded: "as the chapters were ready to be copied she snatched them one by one. She lived to know that the editor wanted to see me" and offered advice on how to behave. Producing the manuscript of *A Maine Hamlet* provided the final bonding between Beam and Bryant. Knowing the circumstances in which Lura Beam wrote her masterpiece has added, for me at least, a new dimension to what already was a powerful reading experience.

A final note on Beam's life. She continued living in the Bronxville house until her own death in 1978. Publishing *A Maine Hamlet* revitalized her writing career. She published the

Bryant biography in 1963 with the title *Bequest from A Life*. Four years later *He Called Them By The Lightning: A Teacher's Odyssey in the Negro South, 1908–1919* came out. It, too, was largely based on memory. Lura Beam, now eighty, then rested on her literary laurels.

The Book

A Maine Hamlet is a gracefully written, non-technical exercise in historical anthropology made memorable by the author's sensitivity toward and fondness for her subject matter. Individuals always respond differently to what they read, but most anyone tempted to start this book likely will finish it and feel rewarded for the effort. It both educates and entertains.

I'm an academic historian, and the following brief observations reflect that professional orientation. First, as history the monograph both impresses and invites criticism. Formal records on New England towns don't contain much documentary evidence about the collective habits and conventions of their inhabitants. Regional fiction, like the novels and stories Beam mentions in the foreword, can guide historical understanding, as can diaries and personal letters. But nothing I've read matches in imagination and richness the overall community portrait presented in *A Maine Hamlet*. Many readers from similar rural New England backgrounds, including my mother and Elena, have said "it rings true," or "she's got it right." That's high praise. Beam's portrait, however, isn't based on what historians would consider very aggressive research. Her main source, childhood memory, is always suspect. When, for example, Beam writes about belief and code she asks us to accept as accurate what she as a teenager observed about adults a half century earlier. That's a reach. Readers may legitimately question whether reach has exceeded grasp. The studies of primitive communities, which may have served as one model for Beam, were all based on detailed field experience. Field experience isn't the same as memory, even memory refreshed by occasional trips back home.

Secondly, Beam's portrait is very clearly influenced by canons of academic social science. Her A.M. was in psychology, she wrote for educators and sociologists, and she knew enough about academic community studies to list it as one of her special interests. *The Single Woman*, Beam's best known previous publication, contained chapters on family, religion, art, and work, all subjects treated systematically in her Marshfield portrait. Students of culture are less preoccupied with governance than students of history: Beam pays little attention to governance in *A Maine Hamlet*. Students of culture thrive on abstract generalization about groups, writing comfortably about "people" and "personality patterns." So does Beam. Much of the book's appeal stems from this willingness to generalize. Collective portraits that convince aren't easy to draw. Beam, as a social scientist, is a very effective artist.

Two more sets of observation. Many autobiographical memoirs about childhood in rural New England fall victim to some combination of romanticism and nostalgia. For the most part *A Maine Hamlet* avoids both pitfalls. I have some trouble with the repeated use of "individualism" as a theme, but that's a minor quibble and the concept still today gets overused in descriptions of Maine. Beam is generally tough-minded. In that very revealing foreword—be sure to read it—she writes, "the hamlet . . . held all the world of pity, terror, love, faith, and fate. . . . Perhaps the neighborhood was not without examples of evil, but that a child never knew of them was a happy way of starting life." One paragraph in the chapter on family begins "life was supposed to be full of repressions and inhibitions" and ends describing the fate of "inhibited women ground down to fatal meekness." Eccentric individuals come across not as colorful "characters" but stunted products of limited circumstance. The chapter on migration makes crystal clear why most youth, both boys and girls, left Marshfield as soon as they could.

My last remarks have to do with audience. When *A Maine Hamlet* came out in 1957 reviewers weren't impressed: one described it condescendingly as "a book for a local market;" another wrote "of Maine and small town interest." Sales were few and I don't think there was a second printing. But since 1957 Maine has experienced a remarkable and still lively literary renaissance. Being primarily "of Maine interest" no longer means soon to be forgotten. Good books about Maine get read in Maine schools, bought by visitors as well as full-time residents, and reviewed thoughtfully. *A Maine Hamlet* has benefited from this revival. Favorable reviews of the Tapley edition, the quality of the book itself, and increased interest in the seacoast's heritage have nudged it toward "classic" status, at least within state borders. This Maine Humanities Council and Maine Historical Society republication should complete the process. Lura Beam now has the audience she's long deserved.

JERE DANIELL
Dartmouth College
August 1999

Contents

NOTE: *All the names except the historic ones are imaginary. With the exception of my grandparents, I have also disguised the appearance and characteristics of people I knew.*

Foreword

THIS BOOK IS ABOUT A PLACE of 227 people, over the ten
years from 1894–1904. It celebrates a cold country, not always in bloom; yet to a child the looks and life were endless
flowers.

Time makes every review romantic, so this one begins
by listing the supporting data of its romanticism. But it
should be understood that even careful studies of American
towns cannot be entirely objective; the sociologist's dreams
move within the statistics.

I lived in this hamlet until I was twelve years old, and I
was related to one household in every three. For the next
five years I lived in the town which was the hamlet's market
center, going home for week-ends and vacations. The most
significant impressions of place and persons were probably
made from my ninth to fourteenth years, but they began
earlier when I was five or so, playing on the floor while the
grown-ups talked above me.

Before I went back in 1953, I made a map of the houses and a list of the inhabitants. Later comparison with the tax books for 1900 showed that I had been able to remember every house and 216 people; those forgotten had lived on the edge of the town and did not go to the same church or school.

Recollection is fairly accurate because at sixteen and seventeen I used to go to every home as errand girl for my father when he was away from home; father was the Tax Collector. Every week I pored over the book of records, planning where to go and whom to see. At those calls, made in the evening or at supper time, I saw all the adults in every family, and saw them under the emotional pressure that makes people eloquent when they part with money.

My impressions of my native place were normally buried, at intervals buried for years. Then unexpectedly, never looking for it, I would come upon some book which made me see individuals, hear their voices and feel the place around me. The book might be about some other race or continent, the writer might be gone long before I was born, but something communicated so intensely that I longed to bring back the people and their hamlet.

In so far as books may be derived from other books, I have read and been influenced by the standard studies of American towns, cities, and rural life, but my chief sources are fiction and poetry. When I was nine, Whittier's "Snowbound," published in 1866, pleased me with the revelation that my own surroundings could be the stuff of poetry. I was still in elementary school when I read Hawthorne's *The Scarlet Letter* and James Whitcomb Riley's *Poems*. In high school years I made the piercing discovery that Sarah Orne Jewett's *The Country of the Pointed Firs* seemed almost exactly what I knew. The other four books

that I read and re-read (1900–1904) because they seemed
mine were: *The Hoosier Schoolmaster* (1871), *Story of a
Country Town* by Edgar Watson Howe (1883), *A New
England Nun* by Mary Wilkins Freeman (1891), and *The
Mill on the Floss* by George Eliot (1860).

My first work had to do with communities and, after I
had begun to think about them, I watched H. Paul Douglass
write his book *The Little Town* (1919). His generaliza-
tions about matters I knew only in concrete detail influenced me, and he told me then that I ought sometime to
write an account of my birthplace.

The actual writing probably came about because Louise
Stevens Bryant, the friend who went with me for a holiday
a few years ago, found the place a revelation. I could have
been melancholy, because so many people I had known
were in the churchyard, but riding beside me was someone
dazzled with new scenes and new meanings. My friend was
born in Paris, France, brought up in New York City, and
had never lived outside of a metropolis; wandering from
village to village and house to house was her first intimate
experience of the earlier American origins. The morning
the car started for New York on Route 1, she said, "Oh,
turn around and drive through the hamlet just once more."

The hamlet impressed me in childhood as a place of
wonder and beauty. It held all the world of pity, terror,
love, faith, and fate. The adults appeared strange, good,
dignified, beautiful, marvelous. Perhaps the neighborhood
was not without examples of evil, but that a child never
knew of them was a happy way of starting life.

The fascination of that isolated day is in its difference
from contemporary culture. No one now struggles every
day for independence, the ancestral heritage, and the neighbor's good opinion. My hamlet used to. It does not explain

very well at a distance, but these people used to be rabidly independent because hereabouts Americans defeated the British in 1775.

A *hamlet*, "a cluster of houses in the country," is defined by the Institute of Social and Religious Research in their population studies as having under 250 people; the next classification is *village*, having 250 to 2,500 people. The United States Census for 1920, taken before cars were widely available, lists 2,619 hamlets with a total population of 461,890. Hamlets of this degree of isolation must be practically gone now.

L.B.

In Memory of
LOUISE STEVENS BRYANT

1

Man and Woman

THE LAND WAS A PASSION, magical in its influence upon human life. It produced people; nothing else at all, except trees and flowers and vegetable harvests. Life ran back and forth, land into people and people back into land, until both were the same.

The two with whom the hamlet's story begins were truly of the land's forming: their origins, upbringing, education, occupations, and course of life were its gifts.

On summer evenings at twilight, I used to sit at the window in Grandma's sitting-room, between Grandma and Grandpa. She rested in a black Boston rocker stenciled on the back with a fruit pattern in green and gold. A little round table beside her held her Bible, a kerosene lamp, her spectacle case, and Dr. Talmadge's sermon from the last Bangor Sunday newspaper.

Grandpa sat a little further back, just looking and talking about new peas and marsh hay to Grandma. He never smoked or drank, and it was only on winter evenings that he read *The Old Farmer's Almanac*, or *The Union*. Both of them sat still, with intervals of silence. They had been up since five o'clock in the morning and had been on their feet all day. The smell of rose petals drying in spices for the winter rose jars filled the drowsy room.

I looked out of the window. The big front dooryard still had white roses. The mown fields where the crows walked dropped over the hill to the marshes where Middle River wound through the valley. Beyond, the roof tops of the town and the white spire of the Congregational Church showed among the trees and, to the east, the broad full darkness of the Machias River. Already the pointed tree-tops on the horizon seemed black.

Inside the quiet room the rocking-chairs, the table with a red cover, the sofa, and the Franklin stove had been in the same places a long time. Grandma had made the rag carpet, the drawn rugs, and the chair cushions in log cabin design. She had collected the books in the hanging book-case, the seashells, the picture of Adam and Eve standing by the Tree of Life, and the illuminated copy of the Lord's Prayer that hung over the mantel. Grandpa had built the fireplace cupboard where I kept my Noah's Ark, with the elephant, lion, tiger, giraffe and all the rest down to the hen and rooster, that had been my mother's when she was a little girl.

My grandparents were then about sixty-eight years old. Both represented well the pioneer Englishmen who had settled the Maine area, laid out the town, fought the Revolution, made the roads, suffered the Civil War, built the church, and filled the schoolhouse with children. They now seem to me to have been stubbornly British in character and temperament, like figures out of Thomas Hardy.

They were the eighth generation from the first English ancestor who came to Massachusetts, and the fourth from the first settled in this Maine spot. They still lived on the original land grant given the settlement by the English Crown. His Revolutionary ancestors were buried five doors away, and hers in a neighboring hamlet.

They had the taste of this past in their mouths. They lived by the weather, by whatever came, and by what they could do with the whole body. They spanned the period 1828–1914, the last couple in the family to touch this rural American life in its undiluted form. All their children migrated and became urban. All their daughters would shiver when riding along little wooded roads, and sigh reflectively, "I hate the country."

The remarkable quality about Grandfather was his ability to adapt his occupation to local changes, an ability which he continued to have to extreme old age. His family was land-rich in lumber, and they had taught him their ways of abundance. When the lumber period ended and they became poor, he was the only one of nine children who continued in the same environment. This staying at home was made possible only by four major occupational shifts.

Grandfather was apprenticed as a young man to his father who was a lumber operator. He knew the great woods when the thick pines rose high and when men lived all winter in the lumber camps in the snow. He worked as a lumberjack on the Mopang and the Plantations and as a log-driver on the rivers. He could break a log jam. After the lumber cycle, he worked for years as a shipyard carpenter, helping build vessels. At off times, he built an ell on his farmhouse, a large barn, sheds and poultry houses, sleds and hayracks. The slopes of his buildings were slow and graceful. Somewhere in him he had absorbed the

Colonial builder's mastery of line and mass. After a while, the shipyard closed down permanently. Grandfather went to work in the town sawmill, and was steadily employed because he could do all five types of sawing operations. He had to drive two and a half miles to the mill, so he used to get up at half-past three in the morning. Three cows were fed, milked, and taken to the pasture half a mile away. Then he harnessed the gray mare Dolly and left, to be in time for the mill whistle at half-past six. In the afternoon, the process was reversed: drive home, go to the pasture for the cows, feed and milk them, come to supper about sunset, shut up the hens, and go to bed at eight.

Once, as a treat, I got up at four o'clock and ate breakfast with Grandpa by lamplight. Oatmeal with heavy cream, fried ham and eggs, fried potatoes, hot biscuits, and straw-berry jam "from the upper field" were on the table, and his dinner-pail was ready. No one ever remarked that this was hard work for a man of sixty-five, but it must have been the reason why he later took to market gardening only, and got up at a Christian hour like five o'clock.

Grandfather hardly knew the word, but in old age he was a specialist. He went in for raising choice varieties of the very earliest farm produce—peas, potatoes, beans, corn, cucumbers, squash, berries and fruit. This was partly pride —he used to get prizes at the County Fair—in being the man who could best outguess the bugs and the weather. The rest of it was pleasure in making things grow. Once a week he carried a load of fresh fruit and vegetables, eggs and butter, to his customers in the town. Never to the general store; that would have been demeaning. He had to be enough in advance of the market to bring extra prices from selected families.

As my grandparents did it, market gardening was an

artistic and scientific occupation. They got great satisfaction out of doing everything as well as they knew how. After Christmas they studied the catalogues and debated amiably about how much land should go into Early Rose potatoes, and where they should plant the corn. They were full of the names and qualities of the various seeds, crop rotation, and the year's experiment with something new. *The Old Farmer's Almanac* and the moon were their tyrants. Root vegetables like potatoes and beets were planted two days before the full moon; peas, beans, and other crops which bore their fruit above the ground, on the day of the new moon.

The preparations for market day were loving and guileless. Some of the finest berries and fruit were put on the bottom of every basket. Every measure was heaped up. Thirteen eggs made a dozen; leaves were laid around the strawberries; sprays heavy with blueberries were laid across the blueberry boxes; presents of fresh horseradish, currants, or an odd cucumber or cabbage were added. In the fall they gave everyone pumpkins for jack-o'-lanterns. Grandma packed these baskets and Grandpa looked them over. Then they looked at each other and he put her grocery list in his top inside pocket.

In winter the work routine was cutting wood. Grandpa cut on every fine day, enough to keep four stoves going, and cords and cords to sell. When I went with him we left early, wrapped in blankets. There were two sleds painted bright blue, usually hitched together like an automobile and trailer, but for smaller operations they were used separately. The wood road, only five or six feet wide between fir and hemlock, was so rocky it was passable with a team only in deep snow. When it opened into a clearing of tree stumps and woodpiles, circled with thick woods, I climbed down and began to play in the snow and make up games, while Grandpa cut trees all day long. When he cut birch for the fireplace, I peeled sheets of the birch bark to make canoes with, and to write letters on. At noon we sat by the fire and thawed out the frozen ham and biscuits, the doughnuts and apple pie, and heated the tea. Going home, we rode high on a load of logs the length of trees. The snow used to have a faint rosy radiance of light from the sunset sky.

Most of the work in Grandfather's life—lumbering, river driving, sawmill operations, carpentering, and haying—involved tools or machinery, or rushing bodies of water. He was a confident man. He never had either accident or injury.

When he was young, he used to conduct Singing School and Dancing School for the neighborhood at the schoolhouse. His copy of one of the songs, "The Mackerel Catchers," shows his thin, delicate handwriting, with curlicues at the tops of the capital letters. His daughters had opened dances with him, and the family albums still have invitations to the New Year's Eve dances of the 1870's:

"——— *and Lady. Supper will be served at midnight.*"
He and Grandma went to dances until they were in their fifties.

When Grandpa was young and wore sideburns he was handsome; but better than handsome, he was a fine piece of structure, a man as good as a tree. In the first daguerreotypes he looked as if he could never be quenched. When he was an old gentleman he looked settled, but as if he had had possibilities, a bit like pictures of Thomas Carlyle. In winter when he drove his sleigh over the snow, he wore a sealskin cap and a very heavy overcoat. A buffalo-fur robe lined with red flannel was tucked around him. A long, knitted scarf shaded from rose to garnet, a piece of Grandmother's knitting, flew out behind. He was fiercely fond of horses. Winter driving must have been one of his big moments.

Loving and watching and speculating about horses was Grandpa's only recreation apart from his family amusements. He had no small vices, no liquor, no tobacco, no coffee, no eating except at mealtime, no personal luxuries —he usually sat in a straight chair—no hurry, ill-temper, or indolence. His serious expletives were "By gorry," and "By Godfrey," and his remonstrance to a child walking the fence above his cherished peonies was only, "Take care, Dardie."

The order was all but perfect on Grandfather's farm. The fields lay between sound stone walls, the house was always painted, the fields fertilized in turn, the gardens cultivated and sprayed for pests. The fruit trees were pruned, the crops rotated, the buildings kept in sparkling repair. Hardly a blade of grass was allowed to grow askew in his big dooryard, and he swept the barn floor the last thing every evening. His barn was neat enough for people to live in; the cows in their stanchions, the horse in a box stall, the harnesses hanging on their hooks.

When it rained he would saw wood, or spend the whole day in one of the sheds, mending harness, milking-stools, whiffletrees, and hoes. He always left the swallows' nests under the barn eaves, and he knew to a day when they would come back in spring. On every winter night his last trip to the barn was with Cyrus the Great under his arm. Cyrus was the big black cat who slept in the haymow and watched the mouseholes.

Grandfather was married when he was twenty-one. He

brought his bride to her new home on the evening of June 21, 1851. The bride had been born in a neighboring hamlet. Her mother had died when she was eleven and her father when she was thirteen, and she had been the housemother for the younger children. This meant that she did housework for a good seventy years. No one ever heard her say she was tired of it.

They rented half a house in the town at first, but soon moved to the country home they lived in always. It was in the hamlet on the ridge of a hill with a superb view in every direction. A gift from Grandfather's father, it was originally a two-room rectangle downstairs with three little upstairs bedrooms, but they had added the ell, the barn, and all the outbuildings. When I first knew it, they had been working over the house and grounds for thirty years. Their homestead had grown to be an expressive and restful home among trees and flowers. It had an almost colonial charm. The chimney was large, the doorlatches iron, the floorboards very wide, the window panes small. Many furnishings had been made by hand, and others after patterns of good cabinetmakers. The parlor had a gray carpet, hooked rugs in flower and geometric designs, walnut and haircloth furniture, lace curtains, an organ, marble-topped tables, Victorian lamps, a mirror set between two windows, seagrasses in silvered glass vases, and always the smell of rose leaves in spices.

Upstairs, the bedrooms had low slanting ceilings, white walls, rag carpets, big white beds, and the smell of lavender and sweetgrass. The grandparents slept downstairs in a maple fourposter, and the bureau and chiffonier were of the 1850 period. The stoves were the heart of the house in winter time, and even the guest room had one.

The kitchen faced the rising sun. It was painted white,

as all the rooms were, but the floor was colonial buff and so were the Windsor chairs. The kitchen had a sofa, very hard but covered with flowery chintz, and a clock with a cheerful face. The woodbox was as large as the closets under the stairs, the stove huge, and the iron teakettle, always hot, puffed lazily.

The pantry, a room now lost to modern houses, was as large as a present-day two-car garage, and it served both as a storehouse and a place where food was prepared. The flour barrel, the white sugar barrel, and the brown sugar firkin were closed off behind the door. Under the shelves, big gray stoneware jugs with blue designs, from the Bennington, Vermont, potteries, held molasses and vinegar. Wall cupboards held the dishes—blue Staffordshire, old goblets, and pressed glass preserve dishes for best, and heavy white ware for every day. Milk was kept in yellow earthenware dishes, on shelves used for milk alone. Thick cream that skimmed in yellowy folds stood in stoneware crocks waiting for the weekly churning. In summer, everything to do with milk was moved downstairs to the cellar.

The woodshed beyond the kitchen was a splendid part of the house; it had all the evidences of country plenty. Enough wood to fill today's large living-rooms was stored to the ceiling; on the floor were piles of kindling. In barrels and chests were meal, corn, oats, fine-feed, and prepared foods for animals and poultry; on shelves, kerosene and tools. In summer the washing was done in the woodshed. In winter, sausages, head cheese, smoked hams, and dried herbs hung from the ceiling. All the root vegetables had their bins in the cellar. Over the woodshed was a child's paradise called "the Open Chamber." Dried camomile, tansy, pennyroyal, and mullein hung along the pillars, and the floor looked like a Curiosity Shop. Articles were stored in the order they had stopped being useful, so that the cradles and baby carriages were under the eaves and the carpet-bags at the head of the stairs.

An old house in those days had delicious smells that have disappeared now, a mingling of wood fires, herbs, food, and the smell of the wood itself. This house was built between 1825 and 1850; it was two miles from the log cabin that had been built for Grandfather's ancestor in 1763.

Around the dooryard, roses and old lilacs ranged; a bleeding-heart plant had grown as big as a barrel; a bush of lad's-love was feathery green, the flower beds ran the length of the house and had sweet-william, phlox, petunias, pinks, pansies, and ragged-ladies. Grandma could never resist a flower and fruit salesman. She grew pears and plums as well as apples, and red, black, and white currants, goose-berries, strawberries, and rhubarb. Just on principle, she had a corner for growing seed, and was always fussing with seed plants of parsnips, carrots, and carroway. Grandma could remember when tomatoes were called "Love Apples" and thought to be poisonous.

The family love for animals and growing things was big enough to include the inanimate. The best stones and ledges in the pasture were named. The backyard had a boulder as big as a Packard, aloof and distinguished in pale gray and rosy granite. This boulder was prized as a land-mark and was called "The Monument."

The tax on the homestead and farm in 1900 was $9.94. It tells a good deal that this farm and the tax were in Grandmother's name. She was a woman dominant without having to make any claims. Whenever she praised her husband's skill as a woodsman, she added softly, "but no judgment about horses."

Grandmother was remarkably versatile. She had only to look at an emergency or a problem to be able to find a way out. She could duplicate any piece of handicraft of the day after examining it. None of her daughters had these abilities. Her life demanded such qualities and theirs did not, so she left them her industry, but took her inventiveness with her.

Grandmother was the last woman of her line to find complete personal expression in her home and in her native environment. All her daughters had to take jobs outside the home before marriage and shift to urban life. She had only the ancient functions of woman, and she never went more than fifteen miles from her birthplace.

Her husband's free gifts to the village were for recreation in the Singing and Dancing Schools. Hers were for illness, birth, and death. She used to be nurse in sickness, midwife in childbirth, and layer-out of the dead. Her next-door neighbor had twelve children and she told me she had helped with the first eleven. When she went to sit up all night with the typhoid patient who lived a mile away, she carried a large white apron, a little black bag of home remedies, and perhaps a cake for the family. As a colonial settlement this place had had no doctor for twelve years. Women learned by experience to handle colds, croup, convulsions, measles, mumps, grippe, whooping-cough, and cuts and sprains, and the tradition lingered.

Grandma had an excellent knack with her hands. She made her own carpets, rugs, quilts, pillows, and counterpanes. She cut and made frocks for the neighborhood children, and she made Grandpa's blue flannel tailored shirts, his nightshirts, and his flowing black silk ties—all without a sewing machine. She knitted the winter stockings, socks, hoods, scarves, and mittens for seven. Her hooked rugs, usually three-and-a-half by five-and-a-half feet—orange, rose, red, and pale violet flowers with pale green leaves, conventionalized on white and edged with grey shading into black—were the product of her recreation. She baked all the bread, pies, and cake eaten by the family for nearly sixty years, smoked the hams, and made the jellies, jams, pickles, and mincemeat.

Grandma was always making preserves or raspberry shrub, or cutting up old tablecloths to make napkins, or rolling newspapers into lamplighter spills to save matches. She liked to dye cloth; it amused her to get a good color. She made salves and perfumes. Her balm-of-Gilead buds, kept in an alcohol solution, were for sore places and lameness. Her little red flannel bags, stuffed with herbs, were heated half a dozen at a time, and used as one would now use an electric pad.

She was very fond of reading. While she rested in the afternoon, she used to re-read her *Pilgrim's Progress*, some of Dickens' novels, a few others like Susan Warner's *The Wide, Wide World*, and some sentimental English stories about dukes and duchesses. She had no notion of harm coming to a child through reading, and I read *East Lynne*, a nineteenth century tear-jerker, and *Robert Elsmere*, then supposed to be a "radical" book about religion, in her house. She never sang when I knew her, but when a snowstorm was coming, she would quote:

> The sun that brief December day
> Rose cheerless over hills of grey . . .

Of all the past, Grandmother talked most about the Civil War. Four of her brothers and brothers-in-law and three of her nephews had been in it. She said it was she who did not want Grandfather to go, because she was so afraid of being left alone with the five children. They scraped up the three hundred dollars to pay a substitute, and he stayed home. She seemed still to feel, in the Nineties, the post-war hardships, when flour was forty dollars a barrel, and the children had no more than an orange and a home-made doll or top for Christmas.

Recreation in this hard-working life was a different need from ours, because the couple were working at something of their own choice, at their own pace, and often they were accountable only to themselves. They never had a vacation. Their tension and relaxation came out of the weather and the seasons. When the thermometer went below zero, and when spring brought the mud to the wagon-wheel hubs, then their daily rhythm would change.

In winter, they gave or went to large family parties at Thanksgiving and Christmas. In summer, they drove out to have Sunday dinner with relatives, with me sitting on a hassock on the floor between them. Driving to the August Camp Meeting and the September Fair, I listened to long conversations about the people in every house we passed. They knew the grandparents of every couple, just whom everyone had married, and what the old ones died of. From the looks of a garden they could name the seed used in the planting.

Perhaps food had more of an aura than it has now. While eating, they used to recount the whole progress of the food they had raised from the seed to the table. Occasionally during every winter, a dish of Indian corn boiled in milk, or cornmeal mush served with cream was cooked. This was food associated with their childhood. The grand-parents eating it would talk about their brothers and sisters, when they left for Minnesota and California, and how this one had liked mush, and another only venison. Except in summer, there was no fresh fruit except apples, but stewed fruit of many kinds belonged with every meal. There was always hot bread, and much more sugar, starch, and fat than are eaten now; more condiments, including some hot stuff called pepper-sauce; never salads; more eggs—a larger volume of food altogether. Only children drank water; tea was the beverage. In the Civil War, the family could not afford coffee and turned to tea; gradually they lost the taste for anything else. In those days, farm people hated milk. Cows were tyrants; cows, death, and taxes conquered all—but it was not necessary to drink them from a glass.

When I knew them, my grandparents never talked about religion, but both of them were members of the Congregational Church from their youth, and they attended it all their days. Grandmother would habitually and meditatively read her Bible. They both talked often and tenderly about the son they had lost at sixteen. In the bookcase there was an old book, *Bear Hunters*, which was marked half-way through, "Harley's last page." Grandfather used to quote the verse they had engraved on his tombstone. The letters cut into the marble in the engraver's odd spacing are still legible:

> For we know that if our
>   earthly house of this
> tabernacle were dissolved
> We have a building of God
> an house not made with hands
> eternal in the heavens.

The grandparents used to laugh when they heard talk of wedding presents. No one gave them a wedding present; not even any food to take to their new home. On that June morning, for their first breakfast, Grandmother made hot biscuits, opened a jar of cranberry sauce she had brought from home, and they washed the food down with hot tea. This was a puckery beginning, but both of them could digest nails all their lives.

They were married for fifty-nine years, and were never separated for a night, except when he was working in lumber camps, but she had no engagement or wedding ring. After they had been married so long that all their children were gone, Grandpa, on their wedding anniversary, gave her a broad, heavily chased gold ring, and they called it their "engagement" ring. About the same time he had made up from gold nuggets a mining brother had sent home from Alaska, a heavy gold circle, and this was the "wedding" ring. The rings came after she had begun to look a little like Queen Victoria, always in black with a bit of white at throat and wrists, and with a bunch of violets nodding in her black bonnet.

Because my father was a sea captain away from home for almost years at a time, the grandparents offered my first laboratory observation of marriage. I understood very early that these two were mysteriously one. I also absorbed from the air the idea that there was some balance of function in marriage. For instance, gossip used to say that in a cold country, you could understand the balance of a marriage if you knew which of a couple got up to start the kitchen fire in January. We knew that Grandpa always got up first, and that this was the way. We accepted it so definitely that we looked down on various respectable old gentlemen we saw at church, because they were known to advise and to operate on the other theory. We also looked down on husbands who called their wives "the Missus" or "my old woman" because Grandpa always called Grandma "Mother" or "Susan."

They made all their garden plans together with evident enjoyment. She prepared the seeds for his planting and he tended all her specialties in a little garden near the strawberry bed. But Grandmother never worked in the garden except to pick fruit or vegetables for dinner, and if she helped with the haying, it meant that rain was threatening.

My parents seemed to have but one purse, and they acted like one person about it. It was a surprise to find that the grandparents had two. Each of them had a small black leather purse that opened with a snap. They were kept in the top bureau drawers in a house that was never locked except when they went to town. But the bureau drawers were separate, and so were the purses. Grandma had all the "butter and eggs money." She used it to buy clothes, gifts, books, medicines and flowers.

Since the grandparents were usually so near to perfection, I remember it the more when they put the apple of knowledge into my hands. On a hot day in August, Grandfather, pitching hay five feet above his head into the hayloft, lost his temper and struck the horse. Grandmother, above him in the loft, pitching hay above her head into the rear, poured out her thoughts about the abuse of animals. That evening they did not speak at the supper table. He passed her his teacup without saying anything, and she filled it and passed it back, also without saying anything. This made me shake; I heard thoughts louder than thunder. I was already nine years old. I kept away from the adults and puzzled alone about this schism. If Grandmother and Grandfather could be divided, nothing in the world was as I had supposed. I could almost have understood it better if the rift had gone on, but in a few days everything was as before. It took a long time to realize that people could come out of their black moments.

They had five children and their theory was that the children should stay at home and go to school, or have an apprenticeship as long as possible, and at twenty-one leave for the city. Of the four who lived to maturity, two walked five miles a day in the 1870's to go to high school, crossing the river on ice in the winter. One girl became a teacher, two went to the Lawrence textile mills, one as a weaver and one as a spinner; the boy learned carpentry and went West. Later, all of them "married well," migrated to New York, Minnesota, and California, and lived to share the roses, vacations, new suburban homes, the furs and matinées, and the trips abroad of the twentieth century's higher level of living. The childless couple willed $15,000 to the State University for Student Loan Funds. The daughters carried on the parents' longevity and lived to eighty-six, eighty-eight, and ninety-nine years.

My grandparents were so balanced and calm in their sixties that I always wished I could have known them when they were young and dancing. The amount of work they did was enough to make any one pause. When I heard them quote the saying, "Root, hog, or die," I always supposed they had made it up. They must have begun housekeeping with candles, for we have their candlesticks and candle snuffers. They had a well only for a short time, until it caved in. After that, Grandpa brought all the water for cooking and drinking from a spring, up a grievously long hill. During the winter he had to carry enough for the cattle, since they never went out in the snow, and at intervals for the horse, too. Grandma did all her washing without a wringer, using water from the rain-barrel.

Grandfather had no farm machinery beyond a plow and a horse-rake, but using the latter he exchanged work with some farmers who owned a mowing machine. Neither of them ever had any paid help, except a few days' labor in haying time. They had come to terms with the monotonous repetition of much manual labor. When he dropped the seed corn into the hill Grandfather used to say:

> One for the blackbird,
> One for the crow,
> One for the cut-worm
> And two to grow.

The wife still did the washing and made the sausage, and the husband still swung the scythe in summer and the axe in winter, until they were past eighty. In old age they simply did less.

They had magnificent health, a hardiness beyond colds and indispositions. The only time I ever knew a doctor to come to the house in the seventeen years I lived with or near them, was when Grandma dislocated her shoulder while catching a hen. She used to say she had to "favor" her rheumatism, but she had only one illness in her long life. Grandfather had no illness until his quiet end from arteriosclerosis.

When Grandmother died, at eighty-two, Grandfather asserted himself violently against his daughters and said, "I shall pay no attention at all to you girls. I will not have Mother buried in the country. She shall be in the town, where the graves have perpetual care." So she was buried there, and he put up a double stone, of gray-white marble, ready for himself. The farm was sold for $1,150 and the furnishings for $100, because all of the children lived too far away to want anything. The widower's share, by the time a mortgage had been paid to the eldest daughter, was $174.64.

Grandfather always seemed lost after Grandmother's

death. She had been his interpretation of life, and as soon as she was gone, there was pain he could never understand. In Grandmother's closet for her best clothes, her daughters found a little hoard of money, mostly in silver, about three hundred dollars. He said, "I never knew about this. Why, Mother knew every penny I ever had, and our bank account was in both our names." His children thought she had been saving for illness or for a surprise, but he always grieved because she had kept a secret from him.

He began a career of long visits to his children. All he really thought about New York was that it was too high. He could hardly bear to look out of an eighth story window. Every time he went downtown, he came back saying, "In that great street, not a soul to speak to, I never can stand it." After he had returned to Maine, he was much taken up with his first great-grandchild. When he was eighty-four and she was three, he went shopping and bought a tiny gold locket and chain for her, saying, "I want she should remember me." He had never owned a watch until the last years. He came home from work all his life by the sun.

What I remember first about my grandparents is that they always wanted a child around. I passed from one lap to the other and barely knew I was changing. When I was four, while Grandma was trimming the Christmas tree, Grandpa was holding me and playing Cat's Cradle until the tree was ready. My parents were young enough to protect themselves; they could snap, "Run away and play, and don't bother me!" The grandparents never gave in. They were superhuman.

Walking with Grandpa in the woods one day, we came across a lake with many white waterlilies. He said, "Do you want them? I doubt if I could swim in that, it would be muddy; but if you do want them, I can knock together a raft and we can float there."

Grandma paid for my first painting lessons, and, after I had watercolors and wanted oils, she gave me a big box of them on my eleventh birthday, at a time when it was a nuisance to order them from Boston. When I saw the paints, I felt myself growing tall and I said, "Now I have everything I want in the world." She said, "It is the first time I ever was able to satisfy anyone's last desire."

When I was away at school, the grandparents together sent me five dollars on my birthday, with the instruction, "Spend it all at once on something you want." This must have been a freedom in spending they had wanted, but never quite dared to take. They had no romanticism at all except a terrible faith in education. Once, when I found Grandmother lying on the sofa, looking out of the window, I asked, "What are you thinking?" She said, "I laid myself down here to think about how we would transplant the peonies, but I got to thinking about the stars. I was wishing I'd had the chance to learn astronomy and to know more about the wonders of the world."

They left their grandchildren the great gift of experience in human goodness and stability. When their eight-year-old great-great-grandchild first heard bits of their story, she said, "Oh, I want to know them. Are they really dead?"

2

Place

THE PLACE SPOKE FIRST of Nature, afterward of living creatures. Beside the strong tree grew the strong man. Along with the human faces came the faces of the arethusa and the violet. The place had grown into the native looks, institutions, and beliefs.

Less than two hundred years ago the land was wilderness. Tree grew against tree and rivers flowed through open sea marshes. When man came, he hewed out a place for himself to stay, but he never cut away the feeling that home lay against the North and the Unknown.

The hamlet scattered around the edge of a shallow green bowl in the hills. Deer Ridge swept around to join Pumpkin Ridge, and the bowl edge around the horizon closed. Forest loomed behind the houses, and the fields in front sloped downhill to pastures, marshes, and river valley. The floor of the bowl was miles of marsh, flat and damp around the twisting curves of river until marsh ran into field and then into lawns of the neighboring town.

North stood forest and south stood the town, and the river flowed out toward the sea, while the upland pastures climbed into thick evergreens. Pointed treetops drew a continuous jagged line against the sky. The forest separated into individual trees only near at hand and in full day. At daybreak it fused into a single dark cloud, and at dusk it turned to black.

The king of trees was the white pine. Once, when it grew six feet across at the base and rose two hundred feet into the air, this tree was the "Mastpine" that the British reserved for the building of the King's ships. Now, pine was second and third growth, standing by the balsam firs, the red spruce, and the tamaracks, lightened by maple and the white trunks of silver birches.

The little oval of civilization, where the town took root on one side of the valley and the hamlet on the other, looked on a two mile view in every direction, except to the north. The main dirt road—the way to town and back again—ran in a loop around the bowl, as if an arm had thrown a lariat and left the curve as it fell. The other road signs, "Hadley Lake, 2 miles" and "Northfield, 10 miles," pointed away from daily travel toward hearsay and dreams.

Roads were known so intimately that, driving home in the dark, a man or even a horse knew just how to avoid a bump or a muddy stretch. Summer dust could be as much as eight inches deep; spring mud in bad spots could catch a person to the knee or a wagon to the hubs.

Within the total landscape, hills went up and down, bridges crossed the rivers, brooks flowed, ponds stood still and stone wall fence patterns separated land into long rectangles. Groves of trees made heavy accents, boulders stood up twice as tall as a man, the railway cut across the marshes in a single straight line. The sweep of the blue rivers, the dark brown earth, and the wavering enrichment of thrusting trees, gave the villager his own provincialism. When he traveled, he could not believe in tawny earth or yellow rivers or round-topped, deciduous trees. He looked at the Platte and the cottonwoods without getting any feeling of a river and trees.

The design of the landscape was happily balanced, mass against space, curve against curve, and dark against light. The pattern was a little like an English landscape, but heavier. The river and the trees were the themes, running through the history and the lives; they were behind the founding, the Great Event, and the daily occupations. The rivers were blue enough to smile, but the Gothic of the trees was dark and unsmiling. Without the sun, the landscape could turn at any moment to forms of sombre and massive resignation.

The colors always before the eyes were strong and definite, green against blue, white to wheat color, grey and black. Seasonal variations ran to amethyst and reds. In the fall, when the wild geese flew over, the marshes turned to tawny red, and maples, never noticed among the summer greenery, turned the hills to yellow, salmon, orange, flame, red to crimson, russet to brown. With cold weather the branches of the silver birch turned the color of dark plums and made purple tones on the faraway hills. In the winter, snow was the lover of this landscape. All except the rim of pine trees returned naturally to white. The memory of this power of drifting whiteness lies in the unconscious, behind even the summer view.

The New Year of man's feeling, which now in metropolitan cities begins after Labor Day, began in the hamlet with Spring. When the fields showed, they first turned from dun to delicate green. The new catkins, the color in the bark, and the first green on the hills came only in April. Just to keep alive during the winter cold was something, and except for the young, January, February, and March were a hibernating period. As the snow melted and patches of dun-colored grass spotted the fields, soon after April Fool's Day, flocks of juncoes flew into the dooryards, the roads turned to mud, and Town Meeting and delivery seemed at hand. The men would come out of the woods, school would open, storm windows and doors would be taken off, the house banking carted away.

The air was wonderfully clear. When clarity gave way to fog in July and August, mist closed in until the view was no farther than the headlights of a car can carry, but most of the time objects stood out in the round and cast deep shadows. From morning to night the light on the river and fields changed so much that it was a wonder the place was the same. The tent of the sky was so large that moonlight was always "bright as day." Darkness outdoors was the softest black, with the only lights coming from distant window-panes.

Living in a big landscape, and feeling the seasons turn, expressed some impersonal harmony, beyond man. The rise and fall of the tidal river washed away some of men's longings, and the woods communicated a sense of growth. The intense cold of the winter pause was liberating too, because when it was cold enough, man was diverted from everything but the struggle. A heavy snow-storm changed the visible world. Instead of seeing two miles, the eye stopped at a few feet and the person was inside his house like the images in the snowstorms inside the glass paperweight on the sitting-room table. Sunsets fading from flame to yellow and encrusted at the cloud edges with gold filigree stretched over the great sky area. Houses on the western hill appeared to have fiery windows and people walking had illuminated faces.

Nothing in the hamlet was very near to anything else, and there was so much free space that everyone spent part of his working life alone. When the pioneers built their homes around the ridge road, they settled anywhere from a city block to half a mile away from the nearest neighbor. If they built the homestead away from the road, the farm lane could be as long as two city blocks.

The Cape Cod farmhouses were set low into the ground over deep cellars. The roofs sloped gently around a big center chimney, or sometimes two side chimneys. Their splendid slope could only come into the carpenter's hand by a skill acquired through generations. Around the house lay a cluster of gray farm buildings with red doors, the biggest being the barn. The houses were mostly white. In summer, the favorite roses around the yard were white; in winter the houses receded into the snow; in all seasons they linked with the white cumulous clouds above them. Grazing casually within the birds' eye view were many cows, usually Jerseys; a few flocks of sheep; many horses drawing farm vehicles or carriages, or carrying riders; a few people walking and others working; and always children on the run.

The church was the largest building, fairly near the center of the hamlet, white, with four little white spires near the corners of the belfry. The two one-room yellow schoolhouses, one for "up the road," the other for "down the road," sat comfortably on their ground.

There were no other public buildings, no sign at all that man needed to buy or trade. This hamlet was only a place where people lived and went to church and school. Yes, and were buried. The main cemetery was beside a grove of trees on a lovely hill picnic ground, the three little private burying-grounds were behind the houses in the fields. But it was a humanized landscape. It had the order of long experience.

The details of the scene repeated in miniature the effect of the whole. The roadside had a negligent charm of its own. Silvery spider webs glistening with dew stretched over the clover and grass carpets of summer; they meant it would not rain that day. The first wild pear blossoms, pearly white with green at the center, hung over the stone walls, and both bloom and fruit of the wild cherry, stag-horn sumach, blueberry, and choke-pear could be gathered along the public way. Small cedar log bridges, no more than three feet wide, crossed little brooks. Watering troughs for horses and springs for people to drink from made anchors where passers-by loafed and talked as they do today in front of stores or at soda fountains. Ponds as big as a church floor lay quiet in summer, except for the jumping trout which made them seem almost like rivers. In winter, the ponds were alive with skaters in red hoods, and they seemed as busy as the Post Office Square.

Stone was the dominant component in the landscape near at hand, as woods dominated the distance. Stone was as familiar as grass. People said that life was "hard as a rock on the rocky road to Dublin!" In the fields and pastures the usual fence was the old stone wall, three or four feet wide. If not stone, the fence was made of long cedar logs as thick as a man's leg, laid in three or four horizontals across uprights at nine foot intervals. Between the fence poles, little stiles were made, big enough for people, too small for cattle or horses.

Wonderful ledges, rocks, and boulders were strewn over the pastures. On the ridge, gray granite ran to peaks. Evergreens opened out around floors of gray granite, just as they did around lakes. Twisted cedars, tiny firs, and ferns grew in the clefts of these floors. Gray lichen, speckled with scarlet and pale green, clung to the rock floor like sea anemones, and dark green moss and plumy grass tops grew where enough pine needles drifted for roots. All the men could build walls and foundations of stone, and people of all ages would rub small rocks in their hands and say, "This one is a beauty." In this period, the home granite was never used in the graveyard; tombstones were of white marble.

Field boulders could be of a shape, color, and size magnificent enough for a royal tomb. Favorite pastures had rocky upthrusts like a little Garden of the Gods, except that the color was gray. One of the best fishing spots was at the bottom of a rock that meandered twelve feet into the air. The blackberry ledges were the elegant roadside drawing-rooms where pickers scratched from blackberrying rested beside full pails. The clothes might be spread to bleach by Square Rocks. The cemetery was by Upper Field Rocks. An old man would personify his pet boulders and say, "I got to mow now around the King; that fellow wants his ground smooth." If a child said, "I climbed Sailor's Rock today," his father would say, "I remember the day I climbed her first," and the mother would ask, "How did you get over the smooth place half-way up?"

Specimen trees were as well known as people. Three different spots had avenues of aromatic balm-of-Gilead. The Old Willow was a way station on the road to town. A single mountain ash, which someone was trying to domesticate, was known to all children as soon as frost turned the berries to the right bitterness. An old man, long dead, was remembered by name because he had planted three English hawthorn trees, always in magnificent flower in spring. The silver birch grove was a place for picnics; the black alder swamp was a Death Valley, a swale where men fought the spread of young alder shoots that threatened every year to take over the fields.

Small living things were accepted as the furnishings of the landscape, and talked about as part of farm possessions. Around farmyards, fields, and pastures, a few small wild animals could be seen any day: the weasel in winter, when he was white and hungry; the fox, skunk, rabbit, and porcupine; the deer once in a while; and in every day's haying, the field mouse with young.

It was only in winter that a change crept over people, and they talked about wild animals. There was a feeling that the four-footed lived unseen in the woods, folded into the protecting snow. Bears, gray wolves, panthers, and catamount were of the vanished past, but after the temperature dropped to fifteen degrees below zero, it seemed as if they could come back. Deer were rare; hunters had to go well back on the ridges. Fox, beaver, muskrat, and mink were trapped. Weasels were trapped whenever possible; they stole into hen houses and sucked the blood from the hens and left them lying in a row. Raccoons, rabbits, bobcats, red squirrels, woodchucks, skunks, and porcupines traveled about freely. Skunks in particular were left alone: one vengeance from a skunk and all the milk, cream, and butter in a neighborhood would be spoiled.

Green or brown snakes and chipmunks lived in places in the stone walls; frogs in the brooks and toads in the garden were known by pet names; bees and hornets were part of summer. The gray spiders under the woodhouse eaves were bogymen for a child to scare himself with; the old evil ones were large enough to cover a silver dollar. The swallows under the barn eaves were as many as a hundred when they made their migratory flight. Woodpeckers lived in the hollow apple trees, partridges scuttled through the undergrowth, and the hummingbird came to the honeysuckle every summer evening.

Among the domestic animals, horses and cows were named by their temperament as well as by their color: Fawn, Royal, Daisy, Slowpoke. Dogs simply were not here, but everyone had a cat, black, yellow, or tiger, looking half-wild as he stalked the birds; his name was likely to be historical or from mythology—Sir Walter Raleigh or Jupiter.

Farm soil was supposed to be good, although stony. It was fertilized with barnyard manure and by plowing in nitrogenous crops. Crop rotation was practiced so that no area was used continuously for the same crop. The vegetable garden between the dooryard and the hayfields lay in rich rows for three hundred feet or more, as broad as it was long. The largest areas were in potatoes, the next in corn. Early and late varieties of peas and beans grew up and matured; carrots, beets, turnips, parsnips, and lettuce made long curly or feathery outlines; cucumbers, cabbages, pumpkins, squash, and rhubarb were set in beds.

Apples sprang up all over the farm, but the best trees were in a compact group in the orchard. Nearby, fenced in from the hens, were the currant and gooseberry bushes and the strawberries. Blueberries, raspberries, and blackberries grew wild over new burns, or in neglected brushpiles; cranberries in bogs and on hills; hops twined on poles near the kitchen door. All these food locations were an extension of the house, and the owners talked of them as they did of their beds and bureaus.

Flowers were blooming for every home, the men digging the beds and the women frequently seeding and tending the plants. The lawn border reserved for flowers and shrubs was over-run with lilacs ten feet high, syringa, weigela, pink moss-roses, hollyhocks, phlox, southernwood, and bleeding-heart. The flower garden, mostly of sweet peas and pansies because they liked the cold climate, was laid out in geometrical beds. There were also big beds of marigold, nasturtium, mignonette, old-fashioned pinks, and ragged-ladies. Sometimes a lawn was hedged with dahlias or tansy. The lawn-mower was alive and four-legged: a calf or a cow was staked out to keep the grass short, and the stakes moved daily.

The woods abounded in bayberry, pokeberry, bracken and other ferns, and in many delicate wild flowers like the twin-sister, false lily-of-the-valley, swamp orchid, indian-pipe, gold-thread, sundew, bunchberry, and partridgeberry. The swamps were marked with lines of blue iris, the pastures with cerise lambkill, hardhack, steeple bush, and goldenrods. The meadows were spattered with daisies, buttercups and clover, blue-eyed grass, and black-eyed Susans. Every wet place grew violets, white and blue; every lake floated yellow and white pond lilies. In spring, around the houses, the bluets, or quaker-ladies (Houstonia), blossomed before the dandelions; in summer, the wild rose covered banks and crowded the hollows.

The grown-ups passed along the flower names and habits, and sometimes the lore about what the roots or fruit were good for. No one ever heard of looking anything up in a flower book, but flowers were the symbol of summer freedom and reprieve from the cold.

In so quiet a place, the air was always full of country sounds. Every hoofbeat of a horse, trotting or walking, every creak of a wooden cart and roll of metal wagon-rim on a rocky road, every cow-bell or sleigh bell carried a long way. Crowing roosters and lowing cattle were recognized two blocks away. The town clock striking the hours and the sawmill whistle for noon carried two miles on a favorable wind; the church bell carried to the hamlet boundaries. Frogs had spells of bonging "ker-chug" in the swamps. The wind could make sounds continuously for days on end. In storms it wailed or roared; in fine weather it sighed in the tamaracks, sobbed in the firs, hissed in the ash, and rustled in the balm-of-Gilead. When a woodsman cut even a small tree, first the beat of the axe drummed, then the tree screamed as it fell, and at last the branches settled to earth with sighs.

On a windy day, the clothes drying on every clothesline made a sharp slapping sound. Even the bending of a field of grain or grass before the wind suggested a poetry of sound which came vaguely to the ears, because it came first to the eyes. Rain had its sound; spring freshets brought the sound of water flowing over little falls; all little brooks had voices.

Bird songs belonged to intervals. The area did not attract song birds for long. Chickadees sang when winter was going, robins when spring was coming, and goldfinches, warblers, and song sparrows often sang in remote places. The crow had been taken into local life as a personality: when a hundred began cawing around an old sentinel tree, their voices were said to be political. Bats were seen once or twice in a summer, birds of legend that might get tangled in women's hair. Canadian wild geese were the beloved migrants. In the fall when they flew high in a V formation toward the South, the flight was a mournful sign of coming cold. In the spring when they headed toward the north, the hamlet, which did not celebrate Easter, acted as if the geese were a symbol of Resurrection. At the first honking, whole families rushed out doors and stood looking and listening as if the triumph were coming from their own throats; spring again, warmth again. The stragglers of the columns soon faded out and the clarion calls ended, but all day long people rejoiced at the miracle and wondered how the geese followed the same flight path year after year.

The hamlet as it lay before the eye was not the only place where the people lived. The psychological area absorbed into life was much larger. First there was the Town, a solid fact, and next the mysterious sense of belonging with Boston. Then there was the sense of intermingling with the woods and its waterways. This land had been virgin forest. Men who had seen its majesty were still living, and there was the feeling that everyone possessed that virgin forest, as he possessed the past. Finally, the landsmen in their little spot felt an impulse from the ocean and from all the remote boundaries which touched unknown territory. County influence was relatively limited, though the town was the County Seat. Feeling for the state was an intense loyalty.

In tradition, front doors opened to the south—to the town—and side doors to the east. The town of 2,000 people, outpost of Boston, was the peak of material and cultural resources. Its houses, history, inhabitants, and events were known by heart. In town there were two falls on the river, one broad and smooth, the other dashing down twenty-five feet between narrow, rocky walls. Their roar gave the sense of power; they were the base of industry, they prepared people for Niagara, perhaps for the twentieth century.

People went to town as often as they could afford it. If they had no other reason, they had always the excuse of inquiring for the mail and, on Thursday, of picking up the newspaper.

At the other extreme was the feeling that life was near the North, and the Unknown. Farmhouse bedrooms looked up toward the woods, and most of the families owned about two miles of northern woods. At the end of their acreage was only public land, not used, not named, not even surveyed. A rocky uphill path between the trees with interlacing boughs led away from each farm to a series of pasture clearings on the Ridge. Here were circles of woodlots turned into pasture after clearing, with ferns growing around every tree stump, and clumps of strawberries, tall blueberries, mulberries, and raspberries. Here rare birds could be seen, and unique flowers. Except for bird songs and the wind, and perhaps the rustle of a horse or cow moving about, the silence was complete. A person going to the north was soon absolutely alone. Every summer's day someone from every house experienced this solitude as he went to the clearings to bring home the cows.

In the second clearing there was no view at all—only woods in every direction. Children would sing "This is the forest primeval," though they knew it was not. The third clearing was called "The Knockadown." A fire had roared through, leaving wraiths of trees, nearly white, and colonies of young poplars with leaves that trembled in the wind. Miles from anybody, it had a different and deeper stillness. It touched the public land that ran on with no more fences, and it gave the feeling that the Universe was mystery and anything could happen.

Yet mystery was from God or Fate, never from man. People felt safe with each other, and menace to property or person was only for other places. Barns and other out-buildings were built with no plan for fastening the door. House doors were locked at night only when the men were away from home. Part of the lovely feeling of safety in the hamlet was the sense of complete security in darkness. Pedestrians walking at night through a wooded stretch of road in "pitch dark" could hear other footsteps faintly, coming nearer and nearer. When they met, they never knew to whom they were saying "good evening," until the other voice replied.

Beyond the fences the public land went on for miles. It had brooks, hills, rivers, lakes, marshes, but no houses, no roads, only trails. Beyond the township the next Plantation to the north had no name, only a number.

The lakes and streams, hills and other features of the vicinity, were named for animals or trees—Otter Lake, Sumac Hill, Oak Point—or had descriptive names—Crooked Pitch, Six Mile Lake, Wigwam Riffles, Great Meadow Riffles, Bobsled Rips—or simple names such as Indian Lake or River's End.

The hamlet must have begun to have its general look by 1800. It had the roads and some homesteads then, and lumber cutting was hollowing out pastures on the uplands. The public buildings, more houses, and more wood clearing would give a pastoral look later, but perhaps no great change would occur. One section of the road remains in 1955 as it was surveyed after 1763, still with no houses on it.

The reason the land stayed hamlet- and town-in-the-forest for so long was that it was so cold and so far from the beaten track. The average temperature was not much above sixty degrees and freezing weather could come any time from mid-October until early May. The County is in the southeastern corner of Maine, as far east as the United States extends. Around it were what then amounted to three fences: to the east, another country, Canada, with the St. Croix River flowing between; to the south, the Atlantic Ocean; and to the north, the woods of Crooked Pitch and Bobsled Rips. The single natural road out was in the fourth direction, west to Boston.

How the external setting works itself into fiber cannot be fathomed; yet just as the urban man walks faster because of the train, the subway, the clock, and his engagements, the rural man's pace has its determinants in the activities of his life. Those who lived in the hamlet were remarkably definite people: everything yes and no, black and white; no hesitation and no shades of gray. It could be more than coincidence that they lived in a landscape of strong and definite colors, with no mauve and no blurred outlines. Legend has them as fairly tough to deal with, and hard at least on the outside; perhaps it was the influence of their familiarity with stone.

The hamlet felt the Atlantic intimately because it was only eight miles to the shore, and because everyone took for his own the stories heard or read about the ocean. Children of those days never took long to learn by heart Felicia Hemans' poem, "The Landing of the Pilgrim Fathers"; they could say it at once, because it was so much like what they knew:

> The breaking waves dashed high
> On a stern and rock-bound coast,
> And the woods against a stormy sky
> Their giant branches tossed.

The child's earliest understanding knew every one of the key words. "Stern and rock-bound," "stormy sky," and

"giant branches tossed" were made out of the substance of
his own country.　Beyond his country was a hazy nimbus
of the State of Maine, with its symbols of the Pine Tree
and the North Star.

3

History

RATTLING OVER a little wooden bridge on his way to town, the countryman slowed his horse so he could look at the signboard marking the site of the beaching of the *Margaretta*, in June 1775. The Americans captured the small armed tender from the British in the first naval battle of the Revolution, and beached her exactly here. Now the river turned into a shallow brown basin beside the road, and sharp-edged grasses ran riot up to the grayed wooden sign.

This long-ago conquering of the enemy had somehow stiffened the life of every individual in the hamlet. "They conquered and so can I." The elders had lived intimately with the Civil War, everyone knew the stories about the pioneer settlement, but the moment of glory was the Revolution. The blaze still held over, burning in adult pride and endowing children with haughty self-confidence. After the determinants of climate and soil, probably the most significant factors in local history were the Revolution, the River, and the acceptance of migration after the Civil War.

The Machias River had been discovered by a French explorer around 1605. To have been on the maps during the period of exploration gave even the residents of 1900 an agreeable feeling of kinship with De Soto's discovery of the Mississippi.

The town appeared under its present name in Governor Bradford's map of New England, 1620-1650. Machias was one of the first towns to depart from the custom of perpetuating English place names. It comes from the Indian word for "bad little falls"—Machissis.

The French settlement soon failed but, in the next century, surveyors looking for lumber, water power, and hay for cattle noted that the site had them all. The founders, sixteen men, two women, and six children—twenty-four persons, but known as "The Sixteen"—sailed up the river and into the harbor in 1763. A few yards from the river bank they built log houses on what is now Main Street, and also a mill, which they divided into sixteen shares.

Lumbering began at once. Until the Revolution, the town was securing its land grant from the Crown, surveying and dividing, giving each head of a family 250 acres of land—"seven rods front, and half-a-mile to marsh, plus five acres of salt marsh"—and working on roads, housing, and town and church organization. The first minister arrived from Princeton Seminary in 1771. There was no doctor and no school, but there were Town Meetings and civil procedure from the beginning. In 1773, a man was fined eight shillings by the Justice of the Peace for "Swearing one profane oath." The settlement grew to eighty families and one hundred single men. The Burnham Town Tav-

ern, a two-story frame building of 1770, hung out its large
painted sign saying "Drink for the thirsty, lodging for the
weary, and good keeping for horses."

Then came the cataclysm that was to unite the townspeople in a tradition of extreme individualism.

The *Margaretta* was a convoy for a vessel down from
Boston after lumber. Machias had just heard of Lexington
and Concord, and men were debating whether they would
let the British have any lumber. Those who would not
agree to ship lumber were refused food by the Tory store-
keeper. The townsfolk were pinched for food except for
fish and deer, but they decided on resistance, women agree-
ing with men. They made a plan for capturing the British
Commander when he came to the Meeting House for Sunday service. The man who drew the lot of taking him was
ready, but the Britisher felt something wrong in the atmosphere, dashed out of a window and got away.

The Colonists put up a "Liberty Pole" in the center of
the town, a very tall tree, stripped except for a tuft of
foliage at the top. The British Commander understood this
language: he sent word that unless the tree were taken
down, he would fire on the town.

Sixty men withdrew to a meeting at which it was pro-
posed that they take the *Margaretta*. They met outdoors
beside a brook and, after they had talked most of the night,
a young man in favor of attack jumped the brook, calling
on all those who believed with him to come to his side.
The story is that every man jumped.

The battle equipment included "a barrel of water, a bag
of biscuits and a few pieces of pork," a few guns, axes,
pitchforks, and scythes. The party sailed down the river
to the junction of the bay with the ocean. Twenty men
boarded the *Margaretta*, and in hand to hand combat they

captured her. On a full tide they floated her up the river, headed her into the basin in the fields, and camouflaged her with trees and branches.

Except for the guns and the scythes, apparently everything was done in the pattern of courtesy. The Commander was wounded and captured in the battle down the bay and he was taken to the Tavern. He had been engaged to marry and there was much sympathy for his fiancée. A man drove long and hard to bring a doctor to him, but it was too late: he died of his wounds, bleeding to death in spite of all they could do. But this was how it happened that within twelve years of the founding a doctor came to live in the settlement.

At this point the first women stepped outside the home sphere long enough to leave a record of their names and some of their deeds. A neighboring hamlet of about a dozen families had sent its men to help in the battle. But after the men had started, the women found some more ammunition and some lead and pewter spoons that could be melted down for bullets. Hannah Weston, seventeen and just married, and fifteen-year-old Rebecca Weston left for the front at once, carrying fifty pounds of ammunition in pillowcases. The two girls carried bread and bear meat for their lunch on the journey. There was no road to follow; only trails blazed on trees. They frequently lost the trail, because they had to feel their way through the woods at night to avoid Indians.

The two Weston girls lived to have large families—one thirteen and the other eight children—and were the great-great-grandmothers of today's older generation in the Machias area. Hannah Weston gave her name to the local chapter of the Daughters of the American Revolution, and lies in a marked grave near the main highway. The Tavern where the British Commander died became, a century and a quarter later, a private home with a dressmaking establishment, and brides who came to try on their wedding dresses would be told how he had died, "here, in this very room." Now the Tavern is a small historical museum, managed by the Hannah Weston Chapter of the Daughters of the American Revolution.

The *Margaretta* went through the war, and was used for some time afterward in coastal trade under the name of *Machias Cruiser*. The men who had boarded and captured the ship continued to live in the area; one who was wounded in the neck drew a pension of eight dollars a month for life. Some of them are buried in private village burial grounds. The brook the men leaped over is still called by the name of Captain Jeremiah O'Brien who led the battle.

The written records of the period are considerable for the time and locality, but there are no songs or poetry to tell the story. Only an obstinate bit of folklore remains: for a hundred-and-twenty-five years no child was ever willing to wear a red coat: "No, red was the British color!"

After the Revolution, the town records say "there was no prosperity until 1820." The peaceable Indians of the area came still to the falls in the river—"Kwapskitchwock" or "canoe no walk 'em"—to fish for salmon. A hundred canoes at a time came to the nearby beaches for ceremonial dances. Hogs still ran at large in the streets; and fish could not be taken "from Friday sunset to Monday sunrise."

The Congregational Church was formally organized, with a policy of membership which said, "People may be admitted to this church without making any public relation of their experience." School districts were organized, the schools began, and a bookstore was opened. The first bridge was built over the river so that travel was no longer dependent on the water. In 1812 a boy of twenty walked the two hundred miles to Boston, fording streams and stopping in homes for food and lodging along the way.

From 1820 to the beginning of the Civil War, the town evolved into a more advanced phase which affected housing, education, industry, and growth. Houses began to express the conventional New England style, with fine doorways and fan windows, furnaces, and water piped in. Farmhouses built about this period had fireplaces six feet broad, with brick ovens for baking at the side. A high school Academy began; the principal was a graduate of Harvard and Andover Theological Seminary. The Congregational Mother Church established two more churches in the area and settled into the present building; and two revivals aided the promotion of the Universalist, Methodist Episcopal and Roman Catholic parishes. A dam was built for the local mills, and, in 1842, a lumber man in the next village built a short railroad (the Whitneyville–Machias Railroad) for hauling lumber a few miles between a mill and the shipping point.

The town began to set off portions of its original land grant into other towns when it reached an estimated population of 2,500. In 1826, two were set off; in 1845, the third; and in 1846, the fourth and last.

The last place to be set off—two and a half miles from the town—was our hamlet. Its independent history began only a half century before the period of which I am writing.

In miniature the story of our hamlet is like the early history of the town. The chief early work was lumbering. Local men were operators and employed local lumberjacks in the northern woods. Houses still standing have wide

floorboards and joists cut from the trees on the home grants.
As soon as the land was cleared, farming became the second occupation.

One Revolutionary War hero of this hamlet was the son of one of "The Sixteen." Jonathan Berry was nine when he came on the sailing vessel, and he lived with his parents in the first log house to be built in the town. As a man, his own home was in the hamlet and his gravestone is in the field behind it to this day. He had thirteen children, and his two sisters nearby had eleven and twelve children. Then Jonathan's children had five houses in a row on the original land grant, and those who first lived there had eight to ten children apiece.

By the time the hamlet became a separate unit, the original family land grant in the valuable main streets of the town had already been sold, and what was left was not enough for all the heirs. The land grants of 1763 lasted just three generations.

When the hamlet took on its independent functions in the 1840's, the fourth generation was on the move again toward the Far West, one to the Gold Rush, others to homesteads in the Middle West and in California. Of Jonathan's youngest son's nine children, only one remained in the home area. The house of this remaining child became the repository of the utensils, dishes, and tools of all his local ancestors. The attic was stuffed with trundle beds, home-made farm tools, the spinning wheel, handwoven counterpanes and samplers, moulds for making candles and the candle snuffers, horn cups and powder horns, snuff-boxes, pewter dishes, wooden tubs and firkins dating back to the 1700's, and very old knives, some even brought to the New World from England in the 1630's.

The Civil War made everybody poor for a long time.

Families were scarred for forty years afterward by the illnesses the fathers brought back, by mortgages, the high cost of bare subsistence, the memories. Yet with recovery a post-Civil War boom came: in 1870 the population was 350, the hamlet had a small sawmill on the upper reaches of the Middle River, a tannery, a general store, and a post office. The Congregational Church was built. Dancing and singing classes for adults were held in the schoolhouse. The two schoolhouses—one for each district—were full of children who walked three or four miles a day. The average household must have had at least seven members.

Within a generation the tannery and sawmill closed; the post office could not produce the minimal mail volume required and the general store closed.

Lumbering was always moving farther away. First it had been in people's backyards, then on the Ridge directly to the north. By the 1890's it was thirty-five to sixty miles away on the unnamed Plantations to the north, by distant rivers and lakes. Lumberjacks drove in on the dirt roads for the first twenty-five miles, but after that there were only the "tote" roads and trails, for use in the hunting season and the winter lumber cutting. On the spring freshets after the ice went out, logs were floated down the river to the very doors of the sawmill.

When the apex of the lumber period was passed, the cycle of employment in the town's shipyards began. By the late 1890's, men worked in the town sawmill which was still under local operation and capital, but farming was the chief support. The resident-owners turned the sawmill and timber over to outside capital in 1900.

A few adventurers had left home in each generation from the time of the forty-niners. During the 1880's, all young

people, girls as well as boys, began to migrate at twenty-
one.

Up to the Civil War period, and perhaps beyond, travel
had been by stagecoach to the nearest large city, and sometimes by mail carrier. During the early 1890's, the chief
way out was by steamboat. In the summer, the *Frank R.
Jones* sailed Wednesdays and Saturdays for Portland and
Boston. Passengers had to drive four miles from the town
and six and a half from the hamlet to the pier. As the cold
weather set in, the steamboat withdrew until the next year,
and people expected to stay at home.

The railroad came across the county in 1896. Farmers
with their families drove in from miles around to see the
first engine and flat cars run through the valley. Trains
with passenger cars followed soon after, and travelers could
see on one side the marshes and uplands of the hamlet, and
on the other the last houses and trees of the town. The
Maine Central Railroad meant jubilation and the New Day.
The morning train brought the mail and the city newspapers, and went on to Canada. The evening train was the
vehicle of hope, the means the young expected to take
sometime to get into the great world; it fled to the west.
In summer the locomotive and three cars came about sunset, and people used to plan to look every evening for its
swift passing.

Automobiles were beginning to go through the hamlet
at rare intervals from 1902 or 1903. Horses reared on their
hind legs at them and men who had learned to drive with
ox teams had to teach their horses to get used to the cars.

In 1900 the hamlet's population still perpetuated the
names of one of The Sixteen, of the first Congregational
minister, and of other first settlers. One of the residents
was the grand-daughter of the fifteen-year-old girl who

traveled through the forest carrying ammunition for the Revolution. Another was married to the grandson of a first settler, a man who, in his youth, had dressed as an Indian and taken part in the Boston Tea Party. He had lain disabled in the hold of a ship in the harbor for twenty-four hours. A hundred years later, the tea taken out of his boots was exhibited in Boston. The neighbors did not need to see the tea. Every day they could see four of his grandsons. Children learned the drama first and the precise facts afterward: "Mother, was it Mr. Lant Crane that went to the Boston Tea Party, or was it his father, or was it his grandfather?"

The Civil War veterans were seen every day, and all of the older people could tell Civil War stories. The middle-aged remembered that when the news of Lee's surrender came through, a woman stopped the impromptu dancing, saying "Think of the South tonight." Several talked of the death of Lincoln and the long funeral train. One man remembered that his father, coming home from work, entered the house and put his dinner-pail on the table without speaking. Then he turned to the mother and said, "Lincoln's been assassinated." Both parents then sat down and cried. The boy was terrified; he was seven and he had never known that adults could cry.

The pioneers, both wars, the westward migration, and the lumber history were all but sewn into the popular background. If a man were so poor that he had no ancestor who stepped off the sailing vessel onto the present Main Street, he could adopt and tell the story of his wife's ancestor, or of some neighbor's. In one or another of the two wars, every family had been a participant, could name names, show possessions, point to graves.

The Hannah and Rebecca Weston story was used to

teach children to be brave. Rebecca had lost heart and cried on the way. Children were told that tears hurt the deed; they must never cry. The single Battle was in everybody's bones: the Liberty Pole, the oppressor's hand, the leap over the brook, the bullets and the scythes, the night sail up the river, the burial of the ship under tree boughs, were part of the local calcium.

The patriotic holidays and the stories told by the grandparents wove the common past into everyday thought and talk. After all, the grandparents had heard their tales from those who had had the real experience. Imagination about the past became mixed up with the realities, but the continuity of events was taken as natural. Anyone who showed no historical awareness was considered deficient. Perhaps this feeling for the past does not exist now, except among people with an historical bent. However, history then was understood in terms of only four waves: exploration, pioneering, Revolution, and Civil War. The movements of church, schools, lumber industry, and housing were little regarded. Transportation was the nearest to a modern marvel, and the passing of the brief period of expansion was mourned.

The area lived in the shadow of the great New England names. The Adams family was known; John Quincy Adams had died within the memory of the older generation. New England writers were known because they had been in school Readers in the parents' day, and because they had lived almost to the present. Longfellow died in 1882, Louisa May Alcott in 1888, Lowell in 1891, Whittier in 1892, Parkman in 1893, and Holmes in 1894. These, especially Longfellow and Whittier, were the standard in literature; their poems were recited on the "Last Day of School," and by children at home.

The favorite New England colleges were Harvard and Bowdoin, Smith and Wellesley; all had alumni in the town. They were thought of as a kind of heaven, stored with privileges beyond all telling, but practically unattainable because of their great cost.

At the turn of the century, the hamlet had lived under its own name only fifty-four years. Older people could remember when it was still a part of the town. Ways had been set in the longer background of eighty-six years together, and the chief difference between town and hamlet during the separation must have been in the sharpening of economic and social status. The town began to take on as much as it could of the habits of cities and wealth, projecting itself as Boston in abridged form. The hamlet began to re-live the town's earlier cycle of being rural, small, and poor. As the hamlet receded from its brief curve of expansion, its people began to develop the characteristics of the minority group.

4

People

THERE WERE 227 people in the hamlet, according to the United States Census of 1900, of whom the writer remembers 216 by looks, name, home, family setting, and reputation; they lived in fifty-one households all of which I had visited. Three families were unknown to me because they lived at the end of the hamlet and were tied to the town, rather than the hamlet, in school, church, and social life.

Most of the people of the hamlet lived together so closely that the collective feeling was like that of the tribal clan or the British regiment. The average American never gets a chance now to know a population unit so deeply homogenous. Schisms and feuds made convolutions within the larger unity, but everyone knew everyone else: what he did, what he had, what he paid, what had happened to him, how he met good and ill. Older citizens knew the younger as the continuing story of their parents and grandparents.

The basic stock was English. Half the households were

descended from and bore the same names as the first settlers. The other households had merely lost the original
names by marriage. What new blood there was usually
had been introduced by the women, because the men were
fastened to their native ground by the inheritance of homesteads. The women who married into the neighborhood
came from adjacent hamlets or from Nova Scotia. The
solitary individual of foreign origin was a middle-aged
Frenchman who had been naturalized when young.

The looks of these people had beauty and distinction.
Only the lack of a recording artist prevents them from
representing their time and place as well as any people rep-
resent time and place in any period. As sculptured figures
in wood or stone they would have had some kinship with
the sculpture of the Middle Ages; their image has so much
the marks of struggle.

One reason the people looked interesting could be that
they were unconscious of their looks. Their mirrors were
sometimes too small to let them see more than their faces.
Superficially, all looked alike, as at conventions business-
men or ministers all have an aura of likeness. They inclined to a tallish, lean type, the men nearing six feet. They
were mostly brown-haired and blue-eyed; black hair and
gray or brown eyes were far enough from the average to
be envied. One family had striking blond children, the
hair gold filaments in the sun; a single girl had red hair
and sherry-colored eyes.

Upon the face of the average young male, Nature laid
a profuse blond mustache. Most men beyond middle age
had curly beards, heavy and long. One man weighed 210
pounds and was tall enough to be in the Grenadier Guards.
Average male weight would run to 165 to 180 pounds and
a woman's to not more than 115 to 135. Middle age brought

an interval of roundness, but age wore the bodies to sparse-ness. Old ladies dried up like birds, nothing left but claws, feathers, and eyes.

In church, where neighbors sat looking at each other for hours, it could be seen that people did not look alike at all. Here sat a tall and ample woman of fine figure, cheeks like a rosy plum, masses of dark hair, wide mouth, large dark eyes. She was known to be generous and her looks came to stand for generosity. In the same pew—church pews were settees twelve feet long—sat a wizened little creature, figure slanted sidewise, thin lips, pale face, pale hair, pale eyes. She was said to be mean; her looks stood for mean-ness. Clearly each person had a revealing different-ness. Concepts of love and goodness and of stinginess and boast-ing were made real by watching the people said to embody these qualities.

Faces were marked with discipline. Foreheads were wrinkled horizontally, and both sexes had long deep lines around the mouth. Women looked intense or enduring or submissive. They wore no make-up, and bonnets took away the softening effect of shadows and let the face stand out without mercy. An occasional face showed a lovely assurance; others looked as if they had come to terms with life sadly and were bearing it.

The great difference between the appearance of these two hundred people and the same number in the adjoining town was in their bodies. In the hamlet hard work had twisted the bodies. Farm life exacted a continuous struggle with the force of gravity. Man struggled most, man's body showed it most. Even young men in the full pride of strength bore an awkwardness and an angularity of motion. Middle-aged men when they stood still took an odd stance, almost as if they were just going to use a shovel or a pitchfork. One shoulder grew higher as the years went on and old men settled as gnarled figures, like old apple trees in a windy field. When they walked, they walked with the legs only, the hands hanging and the trunk immobile. Women's figures were less wrenched by work, except in the hands: hands showed knotted and swollen at the joints, aggravated by the years of family scrubbing and washing.

Perhaps it is because only the adult faces told anything that the adults seemed so much better-looking than the children. Babies and small children were rosy and dimpled enough, but childish allure soon became paler and wore the look of silence. The girls' hair was braided tightly and the boys' hair slicked back against the skull. Choking with tight collars or weighted down with longish frocks and flower-laden hats, children had their own gravity and soon looked like small adults.

They were strong children, always running, skipping, and jumping. Outdoors they were free and rampant, never still. Indoors they were likely to be awkward because never sure of themselves. Inhibitions lowered in the atmosphere. Children were always hearing, "Don't just run; stop and think first." They were pressed to be sober and to "dare to say 'No.' " They were not supposed to handle objects not their own, nor to speak unless spoken to. Exhilaration about the first good report card after the beginning of the school year lasted only long enough to get home and hear, "Good to begin well, better to end well." Girls were forbidden to climb around, told not to cross the legs, not to show the underwear. Boys were nagged with warnings about the broken bones that might follow walking fences and climbing trees. A child's motions as he learned to do housework and farm routine were prescribed for him. But although the motions felt right to the teaching adults, they were not always natural to the learners. The result was that when they were with adults children never showed the fluid drive that is characteristic of today's children. They stammered in motion as anyone does when he wants to act in one way but thinks he should act in another.

After the release from adult supervision, at about nineteen to twenty-one, youth had a period of looking vital and splendid. Young men were handsome; they would be so in any period. Seven of them from one family had the same powerful bodies, rosy cheeks, strong teeth, and bright hair. They were the great-great-great-grandsons of the first minister, the man who had graduated from Princeton before the Revolution.

For just a few years the younger women, taking pains with picture hats and swirling skirts, would emulate the Gibson girl. People came into their maximum good-looks only in middle life, after the desire to conform to style had died. With age, people of both sexes reached the peak of individualism.

Blue seemed to be every woman's favorite color; navy blue wool was the winter standby; white became popular in summer; pink and red were only for children; bright yellow, strong green, orange, and violet were not in the clothing spectrum. In middle age women often changed from navy blue to brown or gray. The next change was to black and to wearing the same clothes for years and years. Victoria still reigned, and at church all women anywhere near her age looked like her. They had the deceptively mild manner, the hair parted in the middle and combed flat back behind the ears, the tight basque with jet or glass buttons, the cameo brooch, the black skirts that swept in the dust, the black bonnet nodding with a bit of mignonette, tied with bows under the chin, and the dotted nose veil. The black gloves were silk or lisle, the black cotton stockings were never seen, the black vici-kid buttoned shoes toed out precisely. There was no purse; women only carried a purse if they were going shopping.

In addition to Queen Victoria, other British types and some American legends appeared also. Beards cut in the styles of Carlyle, Dickens, Matthew Arnold, Gladstone, or Walt Whitman could be seen any Sunday at church. Whole families were perpetuating those square obstinate faces with cold, pale blue eyes, sometimes seen in English country families who have lived four hundred years on the same spot. Even the eccentrics—red-faced, white-bearded, nervy or truculent—captured a fugitive likeness to the prominent. Two men looked like Longfellow and one like Whittier. The best weather prophet looked like William James. One Sunday School Superintendent looked like 1954 pictures of Ernest Hemingway in Africa. A delicate woman with black curls falling around her face resembled Elizabeth Barrett Browning; she had the same large dark eyes and brooding look. Rossetti's fancy would have enshrined one of the faces; and another looked like current photographs of Dame Edith Sitwell.

The schooling produced the effect of literacy in the people. They became literate on the early educational principle of mastering formal drill in subjects never needed much after school days. In the town high school, this mastery was over Latin, algebra and geometry; in the hamlet elementary school it was over spelling and arithmetic.

The theory was that spelling hard words, unlikely to be met outside of a spelling book, rated as important intellectual effort. Young men old enough to work part time would blush if they made mistakes in spelling, even in words no one could define or use. A taste for grammar was cultivated until children enjoyed taking sentences to pieces and parsing every word. They used to do it voluntarily, much as commuters do crossword puzzles.

All pupils memorized poetry and orations, but they had nothing to read in school except the school *Readers*, and little at home. Most of them were hungry for reading matter but had nothing to gnaw on but *Arithmetics*. After they had reviewed arithmetic enough times, older boys and girls worked through two years of algebra.

The one-room rural school gave what was described as "common school education." It "went through" an approximation of the eighth grade. The senior pupils were rather older than eighth graders and put at least the reflection of the late teens into their work. Girls, if they liked the teacher, kept going to school until they were eighteen because they did not want their schooling to end. Boys often attended until the same age.

One or two country children carrying lunch had walked five miles daily to the town high school in the 1870's, crossing Middle River on the ice; but they had promptly migrated to the West. One girl had graduated from a state Normal School in the 1880's and gone to Boston. In the 1890's one boy and by 1900 one girl had attended the town high school, at their own initiative and expense. Two local girls had been Castine Normal School graduates, but they had at once moved to Massachusetts.

The way the hamlet acquired its supports and solaces had little to do with books. Local and New England history became familiar by word of mouth. The message of the landscape and the seasons flowed in through the senses. The fragments of poetry came by ear, either from school or from the old minister's voice. Learning from others was by observation and hearsay. Apprenticeship within the family or with neighbors taught special occupational skills. Any knowledge that was needed was usually available from someone sharing the same life.

It is impossible to know how much cash families handled in a year. It does not mean anything in terms of "cost of living" to say "two or three hundred dollars" because barter was so usual and food and fuel were raised just outside the door. Everyone without exception owned his own house. He usually owned the land where he cut his fuel. He raised any required amount of potatoes, peas, beans, corn, beets, squash, pumpkins, turnips, parsnips, cabbages, cucumbers, apples, pears, and berries. He raised a pig, chickens, and veal, sometimes beef; he always had milk, cream, butter, and eggs. He could work his taxes out in road repairs or sometimes in snow shoveling. Drifts covering eight miles of road to the fence tops had to be shoveled away by hand after every storm. To get the use of more machinery, the farmer exchanged work, both his own and his horses', during the haying and plowing periods.

Barter was long- and well-established. Farm produce and wood were exchanged for flour by the barrel, tea, coffee, sugar, molasses, spices, shoes, cloth, and clothing. The doctor's bill for a long illness might be paid for with wood, a load of hay, or even a horse.

The doctor's fee for a two-mile drive into the country at that time was about $1.50; for a confinement, $15. The wages of the school teacher in the hamlet were $25 to $30 a month for the five months of school. A practical nurse's salary was three dollars a week. A "hired girl" doing general housework, cooking, laundry, and minding the children earned $2.50 a week. A strong day laborer got up to seventy-five cents or one dollar a day, a man with some special skill up to $1.50. Board for the minister and the school teacher in the best homes in the hamlet amounted to three dollars weekly. A good horse sold for $100. A year's subscription to the weekly newspaper cost $1.50 and not all homes thought they could afford it. Music lessons cost twenty-five cents an hour and the teacher would walk a couple of miles to give the lesson. Payment for playing the church organ on Sundays for two services was nominally twenty-five cents, but the girls who could play agreed never to take any money.

The Sears Roebuck Catalogue for 1896 says that potbelly stoves of the kind used in cellars were priced at $2.40; coffee, twelve to thirty-six cents a pound; a pound of rock candy was ten cents; maple syrup was sixty-seven cents for a five-gallon jug; flour in forty-nine pound sacks was one dollar; a man's suit, $9.75; a Columbia four-wheel buggy, $39.90.

Farmers were getting eighteen to twenty-two cents a pound for average butter, twenty-five cents for a superior grade. Eggs plunged around in curves; they could bring forty-eight cents a dozen and they could also bring five cents—the price of two bananas. A loaf of bread at the town bakery cost a nickel, but no one ever bought it because buying made for expensive habits and "If I make it, I know what's in it."

Blueberries grew on every farm in such profusion that the picker got five cents a quart at the store in town and the consumer paid eight cents. No one would trouble to pick them to sell except children who wanted to earn Christmas money. The goal of both boys and girls was to earn a dollar for Christmas spending; this sum would buy presents—at five and ten cents apiece—for the whole family.

Parents did not discuss their money problems before children. It was said to be "common" to talk about money, to show off anything because it cost money, or to ask or tell the price of anything. Even comment about money was a little veiled. It was not said that a man was mean or miserly; he was "near" or he was "a little mite close to the bark."

Children were never paid for help on the farm and they were expected to run errands pleasantly for anyone who asked them. A child was punished for too much interest in rewards or for grasping conduct. A little boy who once accepted a quarter for some berries from summer tourists driving through was sent running across lots to meet the carriage at the turn of the road and give the coin back, "My mother says I must tell you that when I took this, I did not understand. She says we never take money for berries or fruit."

I have asked myself at what point people began to talk about taking care of money. I think it was at ten cents. Five and ten cent pieces made the little pile of silver on the church collection plate. Children tied a penny into their handkerchiefs for the Sunday School collection and a nickel for co-operative school projects, like buying a present for the teacher.

The standard of living was such that not every family had a baby carriage. Some baby carriages, rather like the "surrey with the fringe on top," traveled the roads, but other babies rode in their mother's arms or in a large basket.

Clothes were made to stretch out as an elastic expenditure. After all, the oldest people could remember home-spun and linsey-woolsey, a fabric with linen warp and woolen filling. All children wore hand-me-downs and went barefooted for three or four months. Sooner or later, every girl got her mother's wedding dress made over; first for best, then for school. For adults, the minimum

number of clothes could be: a "best" suit and overcoat for
a man, a "good" dress and coat for a woman, some everyday clothes, enough warm wraps for winter, heavy underwear, rubbers and rubber boots, leggings, scarves, mittens.
Older women always owned fringed shawls: a few beautiful cashmere ones in blue and black, or rose madder, dark
green, and brown, came from England, others were plain
grey or black wool. Winter brought out black hoods for
matrons; for the young, a scarf-like head-covering crocheted
in bright colors and silvery bead trimming which was
called a "fascinator." The maximum expenditure for
clothes was made every season or so at the dressmaker's.

"Fine feathers" were said to make "fine birds," and
women's clothes were a form of social status. When a girl
was sixteen and very clothes conscious, all the men and
boys knew the appropriate rhyme:

> Pride and poverty run a race,
> All around the Jackson place,
> Struck his daughter Polly in the face
> Heigh-o, O-heigho!

Average trousseaux had "three of everything"; affluent
brides had from six to a dozen of "everything." Clothes
lasted for years. When a woman sixty years old bought a
winter coat, it was a momentous undertaking since she
thought it would be her last.

No one ever heard of an allowance, a check-book, or a
budget. Younger couples kept any accumulated money in
the savings bank; older folk were said to keep theirs in a
tin can in the understairs closet. Girls regularly grew up
and married without ever having had any money but what
their parents gave them, and this was even possible for
young men. Considered wildly extravagant were the

women who could not resist a traveling peddler's shrubs and roses and the man who owned both a buggy and an express wagon. He could have done without the buggy—as the small car owner can do without the Packard.

Borrowing money was disapproved of and buying on time—except for houses or land—was unknown. All borrowing was frowned on as too complicated and uncertain. People did not return the same quality of tea or coffee they borrowed, so "Neither a borrower nor a lender be."

No one was poor enough to be "on the town" in the 1890's, although old or sick people had had community aid in earlier periods. Any aged person living alone received continuous gifts of food from neighbors, and help in illness.

In 1900, the total taxes to be raised in the hamlet were $1,307.06, or $6.20 per capita. More than a third went to the State and County, leaving $4.28 per capita for the home budget of $970.68. This sum, less than a thousand dollars, was for "the support of schools and of the poor and for the repair of bridges and ways and other current expenses." In 1900 a third of the houses and land on the tax rolls was in the wife's name. The hamlet was not matriarchal; this recording must have been intended as a protection for the wife if the husband died first, since the average man did not make a will.

The assessed valuation of property stood at half, or less, of its presumed sales value. Taxes began at small sums; a boy's $30 bicycle was assessed at $15 and taxed in his name at thirty-one cents. Women usually owned cows and the tax on a cow was forty-two cents. A farm which seems about in the median position was assessed at $890 and the tax on it was $21.01. The local rich man was assessed at $1800 and taxed $39.94. The largest tax collected was on a large and beautiful white Colonial house, the best house in the village, taxed $47.28.

At a lower level, large houses with grounds and woods, which would be coveted by metropolitan professional people even now, were assessed at $300 to $500 and taxes did not exceed $11. A fine gambrel-roofed house dating back to the Revolution—wide floorboards, small windows, big fireplaces, original doorlatches—was assessed at $230 and taxed $4.78. The living conditions which went with this financial level had dignity and spaciousness. Farm land varied from a few fields to several square miles, but every household owned treasure: a brook, an old corduroy road of logs, a choice boulder, a stand of silver birch, a spring, famous apple trees, or views.

The houses were large. Space allowed for a parlor and usually for a sitting-room as well; a dining-room, kitchen, and pantry; three or four finished bedrooms; an unfinished attic and woodshed; sometimes a summer kitchen. In the backyard, the buildings really began: barn, sheds, wagon houses, poultry houses, privy. In the outbuildings an average of three cows, a horse, a pig, and fifty or more hens were taken care of. Some families had as many as four to six horses and half a dozen cows; only the very poorest had none. The sheds stored wagons, a sleigh, truckcart, hay-rack, plow, sled, mower, and smaller farm implements, with all the equipment demanded for keeping them in repair.

House furnishings were crowded, conventional, abundant. They might have been inherited from as far back as 1800, or they had been bought new last week, so that old and new were mixed: an original slat-back rocker next to the shiniest gold oak. Better houses would go all the way to mahogany and solid silver. Those of less means had less of everything, but sometimes they had pine chests and settles from the earliest days.

The average home had a pump in the house or in the dooryard. An old molasses hogshead made into a rain-barrel stood by every back door to collect the roof drainage. Rain kept it filled. Every wash day, water had to be dipped from the hogshead, carried to the stove tank and boiled, carried back to the washtubs, emptied and carried away.

Probably six houses had no drinking water except what they brought from springs. One well-known spring of 1900 had been in use for over a hundred years. It was down under a hill in a field, farther than a long city block away from the road and from any house. Three families used this spring, each keeping teakettle and stove tanks full of water and holding two twelve-quart pails of drinking water in reserve.

The spring itself was a beautiful spot in a hollow. Water bubbled out of a sandy circle, just big enough to frame a picture of the water-carrier's head and shoulders. The white violets by the path had exactly the same violet penciling every May, year after year; in July the edge of the path was spangled with buttercups and daisies. In the fall, a little hut was put up over the spring and the path to it was shoveled after every snowstorm. Anyone going after water was alone for a little while in splendid spaces of the purest snow.

Garbage and sewage disposal took time during, and were rated as part of, the work routine. The procedures were inconspicuous and careful within their limits. Hardly anything except canned salmon and corned beef was bought in tins then. Newspapers were kept for the pantry shelves and starting the fires; table scraps were down the hens' or pigs' gullets the moment the table was cleared; the kitchen fire burned some rubbish. The little that remained for disposal was taken by a child or by the farmer in a wheelbarrow to a pit in the pasture. Garbage cans were not necessary. When one pit was filled, another was chosen. At intervals the pits were burned out.

Rectangles of an intense greenness about the size of a grave often showed in distant fields, far from dwellings and water. These were the dumping places for excrement. The privy was either in the far end of the woodshed or in an outhouse by itself. The small room had a window, curtained and screened, and was painted. A pail of wood-ashes and a box of lime, to be sprinkled after use of the facilities, stood in the corner. The container beneath the seats was periodically carted out on the drag to a remote field.

Flies were known as carriers of disease, yet flies were common because all barns had manure piles, usually in covered sheds with the front left open. Houses were screened, and housewives fought them with mosquito netting, covers, fly traps, flypaper, swatters, and "shooing" them outdoors.

The health of the community should be considered parallel to the life. A certain occupational type, living under certain conditions, upon a certain sum of money, achieves a certain result in health. Health in the hamlet may have been superior, or people may not have talked about how they felt. The tradition was in favor of endurance and the tight lip. It was still remembered that the forefathers had done without a doctor for twelve years. No one had a major surgical operation in the ten years of my memory. The reason may have been that the only hospital where anyone would have trusted himself to be cut open was some seventy inconvenient miles away; before the railway, this hospital was hardly accessible in winter.

The warrant for thinking that health must have been good is that so few people died; that the doctor came rarely and only for serious illness; that old couples went on doing the work of their farms up into their eighties. No baby died at birth, so far as I know, and certainly no mother. Babies were born at home on the inconvenient low beds, the delivery always by a doctor, with the help of two women, usually relatives or neighbors. I recall twenty-three births in ten years, thirteen boys and ten girls.

The fourteen deaths of the period included five old people dying of strokes, cancer, and pneumonia; two young women dying of tuberculosis; the loss of two babies under one year; three accidental deaths, two in a fire and one a shooting during the hunting season; and two suicides. Both the suicides were middle-aged men. The one who shot himself had been the butcher and it was thought that he became melancholy from years of seeing too much blood. The other, a hard-working man who never seemed able to get ahead of trouble, simply walked into Middle River off his own marshes.

Typhoid fever went through one large family and appeared as an isolated case in another family at the same time. One woman lay in bed or stayed in her room all the time, "poorly," with no announced cause. Tongues could be found which said it was because she had a grown daughter to do the housework and wait on her while she read novels. Children suffered the usual children's diseases; only the mother appeared to pay attention to their measles, mumps, chicken pox, earache, and scarlet fever. People had sprains, deafness, colds, rheumatism, hay fever, and asthma on their own diagnosis and without medical treatment.

Dental problems were chiefly those of extraction. Spectacles, a recognized need, were fitted at the optician's and changed at intervals.

The most acute illnesses of every year occurred in the winter wave of sore throats, colds, and la grippe. Respiratory infection was a plague taken for granted. It could lay families so low that no well person would be on his or her feet to take care of the sick, and they had to depend on neighbors. The great fear of the day was tuberculosis; it held the place of dread that cancer holds now. A grinding worry that took possession annually was fear that the winter colds go "into consumption." The other weakness belonged to the elderly of both sexes; they had a complaint known as "my rheumatism." Indigestion, stomach trouble, and heart disease were barely heard of. Though tight lacing was said to be inexplicable peril, girls never believed it, but lacing seemed to end with girlhood. Nervousness was classified as a moral matter. Women who said "I feel so nervous I could fly" were told they must get hold of themselves.

Two women became insane and were confined in the State Hospital; one after a period of grief following her mother's death and the other at menopause. Older people said that the community had occasionally had an eccentric with what would now be called "delusions of grandeur," but such cases had been looked after at home. Possibly the two women were the first cases of dangerous mental aberration after the state provided for adequate institutional care.

In retrospect, the neighborhood efforts to understand the cause of both mental breakdowns seem highly creditable. The discussions were only speculative, but those taking part had known the parents of these patients and had observed their whole lives. In one way or another, the strains and stresses which broke them could be guessed at. The lay opinion was surprisingly modern; in one case it thought that the patient's mother had kept her too dependent from childhood.

There was a prejudice against "dosing" and men had to feel very low, "sick as a dog," to swallow any medicine at all. A few women who felt embarrassed to go to the family doctor responded to advertisements: Lydia E. Pinkham's Vegetable Compound, Pink Pills for Pale People, or Dr. Pierce's Golden Medical Discovery. The old sometimes accumulated advertised cure-alls and filled the bottom of the closets with the empty bottles. After a death, these bottles were carted to the pit in the pasture and the dead person was spoken of as "a great sufferer."

It may be related to health that the hamlet was singularly without fear of any threats of man. There was fear of visitations by God and invasions by germs, yes; but not of theft nor molestation of the person; not of loss of work, because work usually depended on the self; not of loss of money, because there was little to risk at any time and one could always barter; not even of a villain within the family. Children were allowed to leave home before its restrictions grew too confining and no one ever lived with in-laws unless in the last illness. Living conditions had room enough for space to heal some wounds. Public opinion enforced stability and good behavior.

5

Work

A BOY COMING AROUND THE CORNER of the barn at sunset
with a milkpail in each hand was likely to be singing:

> Work for the night is coming,
> Work through the morning hours,
> Work while the dew is sparkling,
> Work 'midst springing flowers.
>
> Give every flying moment
> Something to keep in store,
> Work for the night is coming,
> When man's work is o'er.

This hymn, shouted by school children, chosen every week
by young people at prayer meeting, harmonized in the
parlor around the organ, was sung so much that everyone
believed it. . . . "Work till the last beam fadeth . . . fadeth
to shine no more."

People were fanatics about work; they lived as if it were

the bread of heaven. The countrymen came from the days when the word "covenant" was used in the indenture of an apprentice for three years. The master covenanted with his hand and seal to "truly and faithfully instruct and teach," and the apprentice covenanted to "truly and faithfully serve." Veterans of these indentures were still around in Town Councils, believing that all work was a kind of covenant.

Work was not for money or for possessions; it was for love, work for work's sake. Any old man too crippled by rheumatism to help on the farm would say, "Got to keep a-going," and shuffle off to saw wood for a widow or to tend the village cemetery.

The Yankee of this time and place was so serious a workman that as a spectator, he tended to identify himself not with the hero, but with substance and techniques. He was good at taking things apart and putting them together again and when his child came home from church he did not say, "How was the minister to-day?" He said "What was the topic of the sermon? What was the text? How many points did the sermon have?" He cared for the sermon apart from the speaker and he wanted the construction of it to build toward a conclusion.

People were on their own as workmen for sixty-odd years, beginning in their late teens and going on as long as health lasted, somewhere between eighty and eighty-five years of age. Before the work history began, children served a long time as helpers. They began to run errands and throw corn to the hens before they went to school, coaxed along on sayings like "If it is worth doing at all, it is worth doing well" and "Buttered bread does not fall into the mouth." Young workers began to be considered off their parents' hands except for shelter from the time they got their first job. At marriage, the parents might help to get them a house. After that, nothing more was given except the mother's help in illness.

An occupational census would have reported every man a farmer. Every man owned and worked a farm and sold produce. The psychology and bent were certainly of the farm, but all the young men and many of the others also worked "in the woods" for some months every winter. Two men were also sea captains at intervals; one man taught school when he could find a place; two had a slaughter house; one did painting, papering, and whitewashing; three or four worked around the sand and gravel holes when construction was going on in the town.

The occupational classification of farming does not give adequate credit to male ability in all kinds of work with wood and to a skill in handicrafts which could devise, make, and mend all the necessities of farm and home operation. Every man was "handy with tools" and was his own carpenter, painter, tinsmith, brick-layer, paper-hanger, fence-mender, and builder of stone walls. There was no community water supply, electricity, telephone, or plumbing. Whatever the needs of the day, the householder expected to improvise a way to meet them. He could dig a well, repair a road, make a bridge and a chimney, mend a stovepipe, a pump, a wagon wheel, a harness, a broken window. He often built a piece of his house: a bay window, a new roof, a poultry or carriage house.

The head of the family provided the fuel for his home. He either owned wood lots and cut on his own land or he traded labor for the privilege of cutting on his neighbor's. The large and prosperous-looking black stoves were always yawning for wood. Cooking was done by wood every day in the year. All winter, a steady fire burned in the kitchen and sitting-room, at intervals two more in the parlor and one bedroom, and a fifth in the cellar only in the coldest weather. Beside each of these stoves a woodbox the size of a trunk gaped; it had to be filled up from the woodhouse supply night and morning.

Cords and cords of wood, sawed and split to stove size and piled to the roof, stood in the ell in a solid block as big as an ample ranch house of today. This hoard of wood represented man's slavery. When a man put a stick on the fire he was handling it for at least the eighth time. He had felled the tree in the woods, cut off the branches, loaded it as a log on a sled and brought it home, unloaded it, sawed it—either alone or as one of two men using a cross-cut saw—split it as necessary, piled it onto the wheelbarrow, trundled it to the woodshed, and stacked it systematically for winter. He or his children would carry it in his arms from the shed to the woodbox. The handsome birch he lowered into the flames might have been handled ten times. The expenditure of time and effort was so tremendous that it dwarfed any idea of small economies. Habit fed the fire with a lavish hand; there was no thought of saving wood or saving father.

A farmer was responsible for the strip of public land between the dirt road and his own property. If this strip were grassy upland, cows staked out could crop it short. If it were a seemly riot of wild roses and blackberries it could be left alone. But if the strip were fifteen feet wide and ran for half a mile, producing nothing but alders, he had to cut every tough green withe every year.

He had to thrash his grain with a flail and winnow the chaff in the wind. His large fields of peas and beans he picked by hand in a bushel basket and stored the yield in the barn; in a spell of bad weather he shelled them by hand. These phases of harvesting were barn occupations. Barns were the men's clubs. Soothed in the dark interiors with the haymows lost up under the roofs, men crouched on milking stools, mended and waxed leather, and talked.

Routine walking from job to job around the farm must have averaged two or three miles every day. Walking was so ingrained in the routine that it became a trance state or even a rest between jobs, like motorists in heavy traffic rest before a red light. Moving over familiar terrain, the walker became hazy in thought and feeling, only turning as a windmill turns. Women seldom "took" walks and they sent their children on errands, but it seemed to the woman that everything a child or a man wanted of her was always half a mile away.

The weekly selling of farm produce in the town was calculated to give the seller prestige as well as money. He sold only his best. Girls sorted the potatoes, throwing aside for the pig or the hens the small rosy ones now served in city restaurants. Boys sorted the corn, keeping poor ears for the cattle; someone eliminated crooked vegetables and small fruit and berries. When the rounded measures were ready, thirteen units made a dozen and the specimens, handled one by one, were of a perfection.

The farmer counted on exchanging day labor with neighbors but he would not take odd jobs in the town. That would have been beneath the dignity of anyone except a boy just starting out. Unless he went into the woods in the winter, he was a self-employed man.

The man provided the shelter, earned the living, and held the initiative. He was always going, doing, lifting, repairing, deciding. Except as his wife planned the garden with him, he planned and executed the farm operations. He bought, sold, and tended the animals, bought and cared for the farm equipment. He remained tied to the daily and seasonal farm routine and taught his children how to fit into it, according to their age. As a citizen, unless he was below the average in ability, he took his turn at helping manage the community. He helped choose the minister and keep the church in repair, leaving the music and the money-raising devices to the women. As a father, he looked after his sons' conduct, but wanted the mother to manage the girls.

The man operated in larger sweeps than the woman, just as the barn was bigger than the house. A man could build a doorstep or plow a field all day; one job at a time. As soon as a woman began to do anything, it split into a lot of unrelated brief operations, all requiring different skills. The demon of function seemed to bring it about that woman should work in a fog of complications. After the man had provided the house and the major furnishings, the woman spent her life in getting the accessories, being responsible for upkeep and replacements, cooking, sewing, washing, churning, cleaning, raising children, nursing the sick, and satisfying everybody every day. For the farm she often took care of the pig and the hens, raised the chickens, perhaps milked one favorite cow.

Every woman was a housewife. In addition to being housekeepers four were teachers, two practical nurses, one a dressmaker, and one a working housekeeper.

To be in the fashion and keep up with the styles in household furnishings was costly in time and effort. Work began with the floor. Home-made rugs or store-bought carpets ran from wall to wall, over which rugs were then laid down as a second covering. Because of the cold, a kitchen might use a braided rug twelve by fifteen feet in winter. Carpet sweepers and vacuum cleaners were unknown; rugs and carpets were kept clean with a broom,

with dampened tea leaves or newspapers, and by beating
them in the dooryard.

The sofas had their cushions of silk or velvet, cut apart
and pieced together again in a pattern. The chairs, plush
or cane, had their crocheted tidies drawn through with satin
ribbon. The mantelpieces were littered with vases, shells,
dried grasses, and pottery; tables were covered with
stereopticons, books, pictures, and plush photograph
albums. If the walls had any pictures, they hung in every
panel of space. The table at any meal had the same profuse
details, as if the woman wanted to make work for herself;
three kinds of pickles, two kinds of bread and pie. The
tablecloths were so large that two feet of heavy damask
hung down all around; to iron them while damp took heavy
pressure from a hot iron.

A housewife served three hearty meals a day, since her
husband and children came home for dinner at noon. She
baked hot breads two or three times a day, cookies, cakes,
and pies every other day, peeled vegetables and stewed
sauces daily. In cold weather she fried doughnuts—sugar,
molasses, or cinnamon—weekly. Her kitchen utensils were
often iron: the teakettle that hummed on the stove, the
frying pans used for every meal, the deep kettles for soups
and stews, the muffin pans. Heavy and hard to keep clean,
they were washed separately and kept in a separate cupboard.

The housewife walked up and down cellar twice for
every meal in summer when food was kept cool in the
cellar on hanging shelves. For the rest of the year, it was
stored around the first floor in the coolest spots; no ice and
no refrigerator.

Winter food depended greatly on the woman's skill in
canning, drying, preserving, pickling, and jelly making.

In the cellarway above the stairs, or on the cellar shelves, jars stood in long rows: pint jars of strawberry and gooseberry jam, quart jars of string beans and peas, two-quart jars of corn. There were stone crocks of Bennington ware full of mincemeat and cranberries and boxes of dried apples. There were also stores of butter and eggs, salted and candled during the summer abundance, to use when the cows went dry and the hens did not lay.

The process of storing up food upset the household routine for days. For preserving highland cranberries, for instance, plans had to be made to get other work out of the way when they came on. The person who went after the cows at night would watch the pasture knolls where the cranberries were reddening and would announce when they were ripe. One or two children then walked two miles up into the woods and gathered a bushel at a time. On the next windy day, someone winnowed them in the breeze and then picked them over by hand. The first stewings were set away in crocks, some were spiced for eating with fish, some were made into jelly, a few were used in cranberry pies and tarts; in all, there were perhaps forty quarts. The last stage was when children set out carrying samples of everything to all the old relatives. The same process went on for bog cranberries, strawberries, raspberries, blackberries, currants, gooseberries; blueberries were a final mass operation. Apples too were handled in quantity, cut into thin circles, strung on long sticks, and dried under mosquito netting in the sun.

Berrying and herb gathering were women's work, done while men were busy haying. Canning and preserving were solitary work, but berry picking was partly a social activity, especially the trips to distant blueberry barrens. Blueberries ran riot on any land which had been burned over in a forest fire from lightning. The landowner would then send around word that anyone might pick all the berries he wanted for home use. A hayrack left from a central point every afternoon and drove deep into the woods. Slow pickers brought back ten quarts by suppertime, fast pickers could bring twenty; fast or slow, everyone brought all the latest gossip.

Soft soap and yeast were made at intervals, butter twice a week during the summer. Dyeing cloth was a part of the process of re-making clothes and making quilts and other household furnishings. Young women used Diamond Dyes. Older women used copperas for yellow, indigo for blue, cochineal for red, and some kind of wood for black.

Washing and ironing were heavy because all the blankets, quilts, and rugs, which would today be dry cleaned, were washed by hand with soap and water. Gallons of water had to be carried around and emptied and the only labor-saving device was a wringer, found only in more prosperous homes. Clothes were cumbersome with frills, and the irons, heated on top of the stove, were heavy. The standard of accomplishment was to have the washing on the line as soon as possible after eight o'clock. Yet a woman doing a big washing or ironing would sing hymns all the morning, beginning with triumphant music like "Hark! the Herald Angels Sing," but becoming more reflective as she grew tired, humming "I Love to Tell the Story."

Older women still held to making most of the family clothes, merely saying to protesting married daughters, "I don't have to run to the store every tack and turn." They had begun to sew as children of eight, making samplers, cross-stitching "Rock of Ages," "Jesus Lover of My Soul," and "God Bless Our Home" onto canvas. For a change they had pieced quilts. Now they made tailored shirts, boys' suits, girls' coats, even overcoats. In summer, families bought several bolts of longcloth. As time permitted, the housewife made sheets, pillowcases, nightdresses, petticoats, drawers, and corset covers.

In the cold weather, women seemed never to stop making things: in the evenings they hemmed dish towels, made holders, fashioned curtains; knitted an afghan, hose, wristlets, scarves, earmuffs, or mittens; after several nights hard work at relining a coat, they would relax and make long newspaper spills to save matches—a holdover from Civil War economies. In the afternoons they settled beside their mending baskets. Among the younger women, there was a tendency to give up all this making and contriving, and sew chiefly at children's clothes and the mending.

The woman's functions still included acquaintance with medicinal herbs and the duty of night nursing for neighbors in cases of serious illness. She expected to look after her own family, and perhaps elderly relatives, in illness. The oldest women were usually the best in emergencies like croup and accidents. It was still a pre-aspirin age, but the knowledge of healing that country women used to possess was drawing to a close.

Herbs were collected in summer, dried and hung in the attic. Pennyroyal grew in every pasture, deliciously aromatic, with bees always cruising around the tiny lavender flowers. A dark brown brew of it was poured down every throat at the beginning of a cold. If the victim gagged at pennyroyal, he was sloshed with ginger tea: "a heaping teaspoon of powdered ginger in a cup of hot water, milk and sugar to taste." Hot water bags were not usual, but hot soapstones, hot irons, and hot hop bags were common substitutes. Hops were dried in the fall and sewn into many red flannel bags about as big as hot water bottles. In case of a chill, a sprain, or a stomach ache, these bags were heated in the oven in relays and packed around the patient. Dried tansy, picked around old houses when the strong yellow blossoms were rank, might be used as well as hops; so also the dry blooms of "life everlasting." Tansy also relieved sprains, and was used for expelling worms in children.

The pale gray-green mullein in the pastures had large flannelly leaves at the bottom. When dried, these leaves had a slightly sedative and narcotic property. Red flannel bags of them were laid upon areas of pain, and were also used to check diarrhea. Sore throat was treated with a burning gargle of vinegar, salt, and red pepper. If the gargle alone could not be trusted, a bandage of salt pork rind and red pepper reinforced it.

Wild cherry bark made a drink for bronchitis, red currants a drink for fever, dandelions a stimulant for the kidneys. Thorn apple was a narcotic for asthma; burdock and elderberries were blood purifiers; sorrel was good for canker sores; tea from birch tree bark was a solvent for kidney stone. Bleeding from cuts was stopped with paper from a hornet's nest. A cold on the chest was treated with mustard laid on a flannel slathered with lard. Recovery from colds was coaxed along with home-made lemon and flaxseed cough medicine and a red flannel armor over chest and back, called a "chest-protector." Some unfortunates never got away from the chest-protector once it had been put on; it was yanked over the head night and morning, in addition to all the rest of the wool underwear. Boneset for fever and camomile for nervousness were other medications. Skunk's grease, figs and senna, sulphur and molasses, Scott's Emulsion, salts, castor oil, witch hazel, rubbing alcohol, arnica, spirits of nitre, and balm-of-Gilead buds in alcohol, were in every medicine cupboard. There was no medicine for a headache: the patient was told to take a walk and not read.

Since families were growing smaller and there was no longer an older child to look after every younger one, the mother's time had to go into looking after her children. Yet as she had time, the woman was supposed to provide cultural embellishments for the family. She taught the children to sing, and to memorize poetry. She advocated organ lessons and built the parlor fire so the child could practice. On winter nights she heard lessons in history and geography while the father taught arithmetic.

When the farmer and his wife had free time between seasons, they spent it in an indeterminate process known as "clearing up," an extension of cleanliness into orderliness. She had to "get at the wood chamber" and he needed to pick the annual crop of rocks out of the fields. The woman also practiced housecleaning room by room and closet by closet, floor by floor and wall by wall, every spring and fall. Both house and barn had rules about "a place for everything and everything in its place." In the year's calendar, work passed in orderly line, varying only according to weather.

The working part of the man-woman partnership always appeared equal; both worked long and hard. The only sign of inequality was in the woman's voice. The man's voice was deep, easy to hear, calming. The woman's, thinner and ascending, sometimes carried a tone of complaint. Inner resistance to something in the life had gone on so long that it was part of her tonal texture.

Children realized early that work was the life-spring. They waked on Monday morning hearing that "tomorrow's Tuesday, next day's Wednesday, the week is half-gone and nothing done yet." To be late to school or church was very nearly a crime. To get to the railway station an hour ahead of time was better than getting there ten minutes early. The slow child was reminded that tardiness was "like the cow's tail—always behind."

By the time a child went to school he could drive the cows to pasture, feed and water the hens, fill the woodbox, and set the table, and of course run the family errands. Boys eight years old helped bed, feed, and water the cows, calves, and pigs, and began to ride and drive the horse around the farm. Girls at that age made beds and dusted, wiped the dishes; in two years more they could polish the steel knives and forks with brick dust, clean the silver, iron the towels, pillowcases and napkins, and be trusted with the care of the house, the fire, the younger children, and putting on the dinner the mother had left prepared for cooking.

Beginning at about the tenth year it was settled that children should do useful work in the morning. In the afternoons they played except during the summer berrying and haying. A boy at ten could drive the horse while his father held the plow, could split kindling with an axe or hatchet. Boys and girls both had learned how to thin out carrots and beets, to weed the garden, pick slugs off the cabbage, tread and rake hay, and pick up potatoes following the man who dug them; girls were able to recognize and pick some herbs and do most of the berrying. By the time they were twelve, the boy could plow under supervision and the girl was learning to cook, beginning with the food she liked best, cake, pie, and fudge. Cookery was hard to do because people teased about the results. Brothers were free with

criticism, singing or whistling it so the grown-ups would
not notice:

> She can bake a cherry pie, quick's a cat can wink his eye,
> But she's too young to be taken from her mother.

For the greater part of their sixty years of work history,
the farmer and his wife subordinated their personality to
working clothes, much as the British farm laborer wore the
smock in an earlier century. When a woman got up she
skewered her long hair into a quick "pug" at the back of
the neck and drew on a long gray or black calico wrapper,
the housecoat of the time. She got out of this uniform after
doing the noon dinner dishes and coiled her hair on top of
her head or in a "figure eight," but the man continued in
the blue work shirt and overalls he put on when he got out
of bed, unless he was going to town. Working clothes
were a sign that the wearer was busy. To take too much
of his time when he wore working clothes was an intrusion.

In the largest sense, the urgency about time and work
must have come out of the climate. The three summer
months raced by in preparation for the five winter months.
Anyone tempted to relax too much was warned by the
look of the sky and a sudden cold wind.

Almost nothing except the weather could interfere with
an individual's plans, but he struggled against time as if
every day were his last. Custom impelled him to be "fore-
handed," to plan ahead, so that a man's thoughts of crops
and a woman's of sewing were in terms of more than one
season. Men wanted to get in the first plowing in the neighborhood, the first haying, to produce the first green vegetables. A man who had not even a watch, who came home
to dinner by the sun, would complain if the meal were not
on the table to the minute, so he could get back to the field.

If he had the horse to consider, his noon hour would be as long as it took the horse to eat properly; if not he started back to his job the minute he got up from the table.

Still the element of choice must have helped mitigate the drudgery. The countryman of the 1890's lived in so large a setting that merely to work in his familiar place gave him a freedom we only have in vacation time. His motions were of the large body muscles, rather than the small ones of eye and hand. Whatever his eyesight was, he used spectacles only for reading. Carrying out his own plans, which had a long period of development, without an employer, without a train or a bus to catch, or a watch to obey, he had an independence reserved in contemporary culture for scientists and artists.

6

Family and Personality Patterns

TWENTY-FIVE of the fifty-one families in the hamlet were descended from five of the eighteenth century colonists. In one of the larger families descended from "The Sixteen," there were two boys bearing the name of the first settler, and three girls named for the first settler's wife. In 1900, six families bore the pioneer surname "Berry," five were named "Smith," four were named "Getchell," and four "Bowker." To tell the several "Brown" families apart, the everyday reference was to "Mrs. Rhoda Oscar," "Mrs. Mary George," and "Jim A—— on the hill." Families with the same name were some degree of cousins, but relationships were so numerous that beyond first cousins they were ignored. Children might know they were cousins to a delightful family, but not that they were equally related to one less delightful.

The 216 people in the hamlet were divided by age: — approximately eighty-three were below twenty-one years;

124 between twenty-one and seventy-five; and nine over seventy-five, including three over ninety. All the adults, except for six single men and six single women thirty years old or more, four widows, and one separated couple who lived in two households, were married.

The average size of each family would statistically be 4.2 persons, but the community possessed more variety than statistics can indicate. Households consisted of anywhere from one quiet solitary individual to a dozen children. The three liveliest families had from ten to fourteen children. Thirteen more families had from six to ten members. Many parents had three children. There were eight couples who never had children; they lived in the orderly stinted houses of the childless. One widow of eighty and one middle-aged man, both the last of their lines, occupied their large homesteads alone. The husband who had withdrawn from his wife built himself a little house on the edge of the woods. Reading and cutting wood, he lived as if he had found Walden Pond.

The work pattern was molded according to the traditional male and female functions. The roles of the sexes were so well defined, and were accepted with such submission, that the hamlet did not have examples of the effeminate man or the masculine woman. Both sexes were helped to stay in line by the code and the taboos.

The taboos were heavier for women and had to do with social status. The woman had to be protected. She could not go to Town Meeting to vote; and for so roughly masculine an affair it was better for her not to go to serve lunch. Within the hamlet she could walk miles to go berrying or, carrying a silk parasol, to go calling. But if the family had a horse, she must never walk to town. Walking would cast a reflection upon the husband who should be able to keep a horse and drive her. For the same reason, she must not work in the garden, except at picturesque tasks, like picking peas at sundown or tending the flowers. She must not do any work in the hayfield except raking the scatters after the hayrack. Only an emergency of health or weather could justify her doing anything borrowed from a man's role.

The man's taboos were concerned with his function as provider. Any noticeable self-indulgence before he met his fixed responsibilities would get him talked about, might affect his getting work, and would injure his standing in the community. To be "talked about" amounted to a vote of censure. It meant a thorough canvas of ancestral shortcomings and current misdeeds; linked together, they could make a legend that could hardly be lived down in a lifetime. Talk was an appalling weapon calculated to keep citizens toeing the straight and narrow.

Romantic love was suggested to the young as a goal in life, long before they were concerned with the future. The suggestion was not by maxim, merely by absorption; it might be only the way the mother or some guest sang "Drink to Me Only with Thine Eyes." Such songs as "In the Gloaming" and "Sweet Alice, Ben Bolt" were household possessions as hymns were; and most children also knew rollicking songs:

> Oh, Shenandoah, I love your daughter,
> I'll take her 'cross yon rolling river . . .

Marriage was supposed to be the way things are. Observation of many couples gave the young a sense of the unity in married life. Children just learning to set a table would lay a knife, fork, and spoon at each place, saying "Father . . . Mother . . . Child."

The marriage ritual exacted the woman's promise to obey but in any home it could be seen that this promise was only a symbol. Everyone knew local dramas of marriage. One that went on for several years was the struggle of a couple with the wife's cancer. The old husband said nothing at all when lightning struck his cow and nothing when his horse fell into a sand hole and had to be shot. When his house burned down he said, "The Lord can take everything else, if He will only spare the woman."

Nevertheless, the community had enough widows and single folk to let it be known that living alone was also possible. Single women were admired for their work. As wage-earners, they appeared more positive personalities, usually of better education and dress than the average housewife. Gossip knew with accuracy why they were single: usually because of the demands of old parents, together with limited chances to meet eligible men. Single men were said to be "cut on the bias"; one was a famous walker, one was a tenor, another followed the horse races. Additional data were wafted around in folk sayings and tunes:

> When I was single, O then, O then,
> When I was single, O then,
> When I was single,
> My money did jingle
> And I wish I was single again.

Children belonging to this society early assumed their apprenticeship to adult life. It was thought that they had a better time than earlier generations, more freedom, more schooling, better clothes, more rights. Their grandmothers had worn "back-boards" to keep the figure straight; their fathers had slept in icy attics where snow drifted through the chinks onto the floor; their own day was almost the millennium.

The sign of change could be seen in given names. The grandparents and those before them had worn all the historic English or Biblical names: Ruth, Mary, Sarah, Hannah, Eunice, Abigail, Elizabeth, Keziah; John, William, Joseph, Thomas, George, Ezra, Nathan, Zephaniah. The very sound of them was associated with Puritan mores and the clearing of the wilderness. They were cut into all the old tombstones: "Betsy, wife of Cephas Stone, aged 22 yrs., 3 mos., 15 days; infant dau., aged 3 days." The newer names were romantic, they often came from books or flowers: Lily, Blanche, Flora, Ivy, Teresa, or Vernal, Leslie, Percy, Austin, Seymour.

Babies in prospect were cherished. New layettes of long dimity dresses, embroidered white flannel petticoats, pink and blue knitted jackets and bootees and blankets, were laid away in special bureau drawers. After the baby came he wore white dresses for a whole year. Then the mother began to say the washing was too much and he went into pale blue chambray. Whether or not to nurse the baby was decided in terms of the mother's convenience; if not nursed, he was brought up on Mellins Food, milk, drinks of water, and nothing else for a long time. Infants were weaned at about nine months by letting them "cry it out." Toilet training was accomplished by praise and by spanks after the first year. Mothers who did not trouble to accomplish these things early were considered neglectful.

School began at the sixth year, but the mother usually taught the child to read after he was about four. She began with words about food and furniture. The name of the kitchen stove was printed in capital letters on the oven door—OAKWOOD; a child, playing around at about that level, learned it, and then began to try to find the letter *o* on the cans of baking powder, soda, salt, and whatever else was on the pantry shelves. Letters were taught separately from a book; syllables were emphasized, because the mother had learned to pronounce words that way.

A child's sins were said by the grown-ups to be growing worse every year, but his punishments were growing lighter. Parents said that they spared the rod because their generation had been punished too much. Whipping was threatened; it was a theory, but it was not practiced. One or two spankings with the hand were the whole history of flogging. The mother scolded, but what the child really dreaded was, "I shall tell your Father." Showing off was an offense which might be punishable by half an hour of sitting still. Destroying clothes and lack of punctuality meant being confined to the dooryard for several days. A lie sent the culprit upstairs to bed in broad daylight, with only bread and water for supper. Very likely the plan for supper at a friend's house tomorrow would be withdrawn.

Children had to sit in straight chairs, must not lean against anything, must not take part in conversation with guests, must say "Yes'm" or "Yes, Mrs. X——." They must remember that "Satan finds mischief for idle hands to do," and must plan their work. The duty most exacted by parents was obedience, prompt obedience without saying anything: "Mother says that as long as I stay in her house, I have to mind her, no difference if I am nearly twenty." It was in the tradition of the parents that the school so stressed the elements of precision—arithmetic, spelling, parsing, being on time.

Life was supposed to be full of repressions and inhibitions. It was "good for them" to repress children. Occasionally, people were proud of breaking the spirit of the young. Girls responded more sensitively to repression, with the result that an inhibited woman ground down to fatal meekness might be admired as refined.

Repression was the more rigorous because it had to teach necessities of conduct, such as the need of caution in handling fire, sharp-edged tools, boiling water, and the lamp. The cautions about fire were very effective. Households burned wood every day and at least one or two lamps every evening, yet only one fire happened in ten years. It caught from the explosion of an oil stove. Girls of nine were trusted to carry lamps from room to room and their brothers used the axe and hatchet as they wished, without serious accident. Boys were not allowed firearms until their late teens. Since rabbits and squirrels were never eaten and deer were the chief hunting interest, the cost of the license may have influenced this custom.

In spite of the theories about better times for the young, a child was not supposed to have any particular rights outside of his keep, clothes, health, and schooling. Until he chose his own life-work, he was an extension of his parents' personality. Adults talked over theories of discipline and usually tried them out at length on the first child. The later offspring were left more to themselves. "No" and "Be careful" as prohibitions about the dangers of life easily were extended to other commands, ensuring the carrying of rubbers and raincoat as well as controlling the childish imprudence of every hour. Children noticed that if a parent said something hastily, he hardly ever backed down after he cooled off.

Even before school days began, different behavior was taught to the girls and the boys. The very toys provided, after the rattle with bells and the rubber cat were outgrown, were geared to the adult roles each child would have to fill. Boys had few toys; stuffed animals when small, then tops and little carts and wagons, and then bats and balls. It would not have been possible for a girl to get any rocking-horse to sit astride, nor any stuffed animal such as a lion or a tiger; these would only be for a boy. Both sexes, however, had hoops, sleds, skates and fishing rods, perhaps kites; rarely a tricycle or bicycle or the use of a horse.

Girls had a fearful abundance of toys to look after and take care of, beginning with any number of dolls, say twenty, to be named, dressed and dandled, and wheeled about in the doll carriage. Their sets of dishes had little plates, cups and saucers, sugar bowl and cream pitcher, coffee pot and chocolate pot big enough to eat from, and a miss ten years old would say, "Mine is Haviland, Aunt So-and-So sent it from Boston." Their alluring little stoves with frying pans and tea kettles were an introduction to the years of cooking and dishwashing to come. The dolls had beds, with sheets and bed-covering to be washed and ironed; another glimpse of the future. Dolls required dress-making, so the child owner wanted a mending basket and piece-bag.

One girl had a Negro doll three feet tall, made by some grandmother who remembered other days. Dinah was shiny black cloth, with brown lamb's wool for hair and big hoop ear-rings; her frock was red and black checked wool, with a lace collar, a yellow necktie, and a white apron. No one knew how to play with her; she was a Civil War museum piece in a rocking chair.

Some girls were never allowed to play with boys. A girl heard early that she must not climb around or be rough. She had to sit up straight on her sled; only boys and tom-boys went belly-whopping down the hills. One of the levers for the female was "Whistling girls and crowing hens, always come to some bad end." The real unfortunate was a boy with a sister a few years younger; he had to think all the time about "your little Sister" and measure what he wanted to do by her good.

It was always better for the female to be reluctant: "When Mr. Lawson asked me to marry him, he did it by letter. I acknowledged his letter at once, but all I said was that I thanked him for the honor and I would take three weeks to think over his proposal. At the end of the three weeks I wrote again and said I accepted." "But, Mrs. Lawson, didn't you really know before the three weeks?" "Yes, child, I knew, but it does not do for girls to be forward."

Father, Grandfather and Big Brother had to be waited on and it used to be noted that men must never be delayed; everything they were doing was important. Still it was considered abnormal when a family or a mother showed partiality to boys. It was almost a gospel that all children have equal clothes, gifts, and opportunity. Girls were helped to make plans to earn money, have work, and travel, just as boys were. The favoritism most oppressive to children was the rule of primogeniture. Parents said, "The younger must defer to the elder," and this saying could be twisted to cover many situations. The first child perhaps stood for the parents' youthful optimism; he often seemed to get the best of everything.

Because children's fears have been better understood in the twentieth century, it would be interesting to know what country children were afraid of in this environment. They were not afraid of the dark or of the woods. After an interval in babyhood, they were not afraid of strangers except Indians. They did not mind being left alone in the house. They were not really afraid of punishment, because it amounted to so little; they did not fear animals; they said, "There aren't any ghosts."

Yet children knew fear. In play they often wanted to feel fear. They imagined fears in which their lives were in danger. Maine does not have poisonous snakes, but it chilled the blood to call every snake poisonous. If the child were an explorer riding in the tropics, every garter snake was a boa constrictor, and horse and child got away by the skin of the teeth. A striped snake was a rattler, a spider was a tarantula, an ant a scorpion, and an ant hill was the territory of scorpions. A swamp was a quicksand. As soon as the foot went in an inch, children began the long slow luxury of pretending that the suction was up to the knees, up to the waist, approaching the armpits. The woods had special haunts for bears, lions, tigers, and leopards, and the hunters, perhaps dragging the house cat for vividness, contrived scenes of deadly peril from tooth and claw. It was necessary to have blood; cranberry sauce stolen from the family jar made splendid gore. Parents forbade binding at the stake, but children stood beside the clothes post and played that they were bound in an Indian camp. Indian raids and imprisonment facing torture were so violent that the child almost became really afraid of his own fantasy.

The child's symbols of cruelty and power in those days were probably the mowing machine and the hawk. The red mower was beautiful in action, made a sound like a great bee, looked splendid, and cut swathes faster than a man. It was because of prohibitions often repeated that the mower began to seem relentless. The mower was machinery and to go near machinery was strictly forbidden. A serious accident of long ago was made into a folk tale until feet and hands dreaded the sharp teeth and long blade. The machine seemed to be stronger than people and could make blood stream.

The hawk was the agent in the child's first tragedy outside himself. When spring grew warm and everything was relaxing in the sun, the mother hens with their broods of chicks began to live in barrels cushioned with hay in the backyard. Three or four barrels lay on their sides with feeding pans, water dishes, and all the trappings of home. The mother hens went around scratching and clucking, the yellow chickens ran and cheeped and took little drinks of water. Children used to watch the scene and invent games about it. Then suddenly, one day the hawk dropped from the sky and flew up with a chicken in its talons. The cries that followed came not only from the mother hens, but also from the big poultry yard; clearly the hens knew. After this, children watched, and if the hawk came circling they ran to shut the chickens into the barrels. But something about this drop from the sky suggested that hawks fell on everybody and not just on chickens. The helplessness of man in the hawk-and-chicken situation was different from the cat-with-mouse or cat-with-bird situation. These were not tragedies probably because the child could do something about them. He took the prey away from the cat and often it lived; if it were already dead, he buried it with ceremonies in his bird-and-animal graveyard on the side of the hill.

The child extended his fear of the mower to the sawmill. He had never been inside it, but he often drove by the open doors. The loud whirring of the saws was matched by the screams of the lumber. With his gifted imagination making dangerous things more dangerous and sharp things sharper, he felt the saws as a magnified mowing machine, threatening the men at work.

The community mourning at death probably gave the first thoughts about fate and the acceptance of the inevitable. A girl of seventeen and a young man of twenty-one died during the period when I was close to the hamlet. Month after month went by while this girl was dying of tuberculosis. Her temperature, her appetite, the flush on her cheek, her hope to get well enough to go back to school, were talked of in the neighborhood every day. The boy, out hunting, was shot by another hunter; "wearing a bright red sweater, he was, but still. . . ." The adults who usually seemed so resourceful and were the models for conduct, in grief showed their uncertainty. They said too much; children listened, understood that no one could do anything, and grew a little older.

The community attitude toward children was not "progressive" in today's sense, but the seeds of modernity were in it. Attitude toward old age, on the other hand, was squarely opposed to that which has been hardening nationally for the last twenty-five years. The old counted as active members of society. They were deferred to, because while leading the same kind of life everyone else did, they had gained in tolerance and wisdom. Their children had usually migrated, so they had to lead relatively active lives. They took longer to do less, but they were still running their own farms and earning their own way. Old men close to eighty went away alone, in winter to cut wood, in summer to the fields carrying a scythe. Their wives were still cooking hearty dinners after doing a forenoon's washing. Only two of the town's elderly were past work; the old lady by the fire was over ninety and the old gentleman had sons who had taken over his functions. The rest went on with their diminishing lives as they had to, until within a few weeks of the deathbed. They retained alertness in things they were really interested in and never appeared vegetative as old people do in metropolitan Homes for the Aged. In fact, the old people were stimulating. Their looks, mentality, work, and endurance told such stories that the young thought of them as people of stature.

In old age, in summer, and in the woods, it was possible to develop patterns of solitude. But from October to May solitude was not possible. No matter how roomy the house, everyone was in the rooms where the fires were. The literal closeness of the family in the coldest weather came to be taken for granted, as the people now in urban slums accept one-room apartments. The kitchen was also the living-room. On any February morning, the mother was standing over the stove making a hot potato-and-meal mash for the hens; one daughter was making cookies at a side table, and another was cleaning lamps. A boy sat by the fire mending his traps and the father kept going in and out thawing frozen pipes. In the evening the same group sat around in the same room at leisure occupations, reading, painting, studying, doing something with the hands.

The closeness of the household explains why the help had to be a part of the family. In the whole area, no one was called a servant. Resistance to the idea of menial position was a principle. In the hamlet, hired help was only temporary. When the mother was sick, a widow, a spinster, or a neighbor's daughter came, lived as a member of the household and got about $2.00 a week. If the same person went to work in town, she took care to be "help" to an old couple or an invalid and she would not take the position unless she ate with the family. Not to eat with the family would mean dropping to the "hired girl" status, a lower class. No one from the hamlet would accept this status. The few women who did came from even more remote rural places and formed a special pariah caste; they went around only with each other.

A society so compact and familiar, without the influence of books, theater, travel, and national news, also needed strangeness. Ways were made for being in touch with personality outside the family and beyond the hamlet. The community was not learned enough in the Bible to lean on Old Testament figures. It never imagined the mythical lumberjacks invented in some lumber regions. No heroes towered except Washington and Lincoln. War heroes of the Revolution and a few of the original settlers were legendary, but they were so well-known that nothing new was left. No contemporary was talked of much except the Dark Horse, James G. Blaine, and after San Juan Hill, Theodore Roosevelt. For its real admiration and pattern, the hamlet selected some of its own living personalities, characters who stood up under daily scrutiny.

Gossip would explore the ideal of a good man. Many men were considered pretty good and no man at all was thought to be really bad, but one man was pointed out as the ideal for children of both sexes to take. He was a one-time lumberman turned farmer, a modest and stable man with a wife, but no children. The hamlet was his child. He worked for its welfare through the local institutions, the church, the school, the Town Meeting, and in town through the groups in the grocery store. Said to be always on the side of progress and the right, he was somehow unable to bore people or tire them out. In 1955, the newspapers said about Clement Attlee of England the kind of things that used to be said about Deacon Smith.

The model woman was more striking. Compared with the average, she was exotic. A single woman in the late twenties, beautiful, dignified, rather retiring, she lived at home with old parents. She taught school, taught Sunday School classes, played the church organ, sang well. Farm women looked up to her, not because she was a teacher, but because of her looks and her ability to invest every day with a larger meaning. Girls admired her curly hair, her clothes, her manners, her speaking voice. Because they knew that she read Browning—this was told on the blueberry barrens—they intended to read Browning as soon as they could get hold of a book. Boys had crushes on her from the time they entered the teens until they had sweethearts of their own. Men used to say, "No man is good enough for her." She was a "Mary" type, the gentle woman who did something by just being herself.

There was also a "Martha," a woman of wonderful community spirit, much admired. She was a middle-aged woman in a Paisley shawl and black bonnet, who drove her own horse around when she made calls. Women who had never learned to drive, who were timid and had little to say outside of their own homes, were willing to follow her. She kept a fine house and had beautiful children, but she also made it a duty to promote church and school affairs, better roads, and good times for young people. Memorial and Independence Day celebrations were planned by this woman; she saw to it that hayracks were provided for those who had no conveyance, that arrangements were seemly, and that amusements included all ages.

Apart from individuals, the community praised certain families as units and took them as models. The average family was almost too hardworking and decorous. That meagerness was undesirable was implied in the popularity of a family of abundant and bounding life. The favorite family had twelve children. The father was a huge man who had fought at Gettysburg. He had so many boys that he had his own crew for cutting wood and all kinds of help for farming. His barns spilled over with horses, cattle, hay, and machinery. The mother could get a rig to go calling with on the minute. The house was full of girls and canaries. Their great vegetable gardens had rows of prize dahlias. This couple would give parties on the slightest provocation and their daughters' trousseaux and weddings were local milestones.

Other families who set standards had sometimes lived "away" and returned home, or they had fine children who had migrated out of the area but came home every summer to add lustre to the parents. The hamlet also had its types of the rich man, the boaster, the invalid woman, the independent woman, the morose bachelor, and the youthful Apollo. They were not patterns; they were information. All conspicuous people struck deep into popular thinking and must be thought of as an extension of family influence. Prominence brought them more publicity by word of mouth than can now be paid for through a publicity agent.

The adjacent town, which everyone knew well, offered additional sources for personality patterns. The three doctors, for example, held themselves aloof and were venerated. All had good training for the period and all were dedicated to their profession. The two lawyers were not liked for anything but their wits, but men used to attend court to hear them cross-examine. The two entrepreneurs were in lumber. One of them, "Old J. K.," was very popular. His astuteness, his work history, and his methods were absorbed as part of the spectacle of creation. It was said that when he died the town might just come to an end.

Store keepers were sniffed at; very selfish men; no higher ambition than to rub two coins together. They helped to set a pattern, one of steady work and long hours. Work in the town was not quite as everlasting as that in the country, but it was long. Stores opened in the morning by half past seven or eight o'clock and closed at six o'clock. The older merchants were sometimes men who had served a three-year apprenticeship to a trade at $40 to $60 a year, and they were craftsmen before they became store owners. They were proud of never having had a vacation and never needing one. Holidays were well enough, but a week's vacation was a sign of the degeneracy of the times.

If a child resisted the family patterns or could not find what seemed natural to him close at hand, he still had all the examples of the community and the town before him. If he preferred ideas to people, the church and school offered other patterns, and he could frame choices from theory or could mingle theory and practice.

7

Church

"THE HEAVEN'S DECLARE the glory of God and the firmament sheweth His handiwork. . . . And I saw a new heaven and a new earth; for the first heaven and the first earth are passed away."

The old minister who knelt in prayer before he turned to face the congregation brought each Sunday that he came to the hamlet a statement about the glory of God and the newness of life. The church came into the lives of the people for only eight weeks in summer, and it came through his voice. Full, musical, disembodied, selfless, the voice told stories, taught lessons, read the Scriptures, and opened the world of learning and imagination.

The minister had been graduated from a college and a Theological Seminary when he was ordained in 1855. Thus he was schooled beyond the average for his time. He came to the area when he was young, nurtured in the liberal tradition of the day. His beliefs were severely questioned and the Council which examined him on his faith almost refused to ordain him. He married a daughter of the colonist who led the battle of the *Margaretta*, and he spent all his life in the state: thirty-four years in nearby towns and, after that, he conducted services in villages and hamlets as long as he could hold his buggy reins. Each Sunday afternoon during July and August, after he had preached in a neighboring village in the morning, he drove to the hamlet. Shepherding this New England community for only eight weeks of the year was a hard assignment and he was already nearly seventy years old.

The pastor never came to Sunday School or prayer meeting, did not concern himself with the music, paid no calls on the parish. His contacts beyond the pulpit stopped when he had shaken hands at the church door. Nevertheless, he suited the place. He looked like the people's beliefs. Fortitude was prized and the old man had it. He stood erect and his face had taken on the look of one who has struggled but not given way; it was granite in the sun and fully set apart. No oratory and no gestures, but he was full of the Bible and his voice could ring all the bells of sound. As a minister, he simply showed these qualities to his flock. He seemed never to try to move an audience. He limited his range to teaching, binding humanity in social ceremonial and releasing individual personality.

Every summer he read aloud a great number of Bible stories, stories that began with "Now it came to pass" and went on until he said, "The words of Job are ended." He read two lessons and preached from a text repeated often enough to linger in memory. His sermons were built firmly, the listener could follow the development from the beginning to the cadence of the end. He covered the main events in the life of Christ, the Psalms, the Book of Revelations, and various stories of rural life every season. In alternate years he discussed phases of the Old Testament. His stories and illustrations of principles always came from the Bible. No matter what the concrete examples in the farm life and trading going on around him, he translated thought and image into the religious framework of long ago. The church hour was rich with ancient cities and seas, prophets, and exotic trees and fruits; his people wore Biblical clothes and spoke with other tongues.

His congregation used to go home and look up in the Concordance these accounts of temples and palaces, altars and chariots, prophets and shepherds. In prayer meeting by themselves, they used to speak of Saul made Paul, Ruth and Boaz, Samson and Delilah, and the two baskets of figs set before the temple of Jehovah.

These services in the summer were almost all there was of church life. No member was received into the church in a decade, no baby was christened, no marriage solemnized in the building. The church did not make use of its demominational connections or of the mechanics of growth upon which churches rely. A bequest provided most of the budget, so the church lacked the discipline of giving or even of full self-support. But the church was the focus of intellectual life. Everyone went to church except three or four men who turned out only for funerals and the hamlet kept both the Bible and the preaching well in mind.

Every family owned a Bible. Every child, as soon as he could read well, received a Bible marked "From Father and Mother," with the date of the Christmas or birthday on the flyleaf. On winter evenings, people with a taste for reading returned again and again to the Bible. To "read the Bible through" in three or four winters was an ambition of young people and some of them, complaining of the duller portions, actually did so. Families took city newspapers for "Dr. Talmadge's Sermon" and his sermon for the last Sunday lay on the sitting-room table.

The white church was founded in 1871 with twenty-six members, and it stood in the center of the hamlet. Extraordinary influence came from its ecclesiastical architecture. The building was considered beautiful, majestic, and holy. Most of the people had known this church first in childhood, when everything looks large. In old age it could still have been the largest place they knew well. They might have gone to church in town, but they felt townspeople looked down upon them. They stayed at home, therefore, and that law of aesthetics which draws up the human being's maximum response to the best art he knows worked in them. The architecture of the church evoked in the worshipper the same kind of feeling that comes in St. Paul's or Chartres.

The church was the shrine and the metallic churchbell rang over the pastures as if it were chimes. When there was an evening service, sound floated alive along with the sunset clouds. The four turrets on the belfry—like clumsy treetops cut in wood—laid the basis for illogical and persistent notions about the Gothic.

The church gave most of the people their first ideas of design and form on a scale larger than a private house, and was, with school and Town Meeting, their only contact with social ceremonial. It united them in a collective experience, introduced them to each other on the Sunday plane, and offered some opportunity for adult education. It required that they free the self from complete dependence on the literal and take some position within themselves on the Unseen.

The inside of the church seemed very large after farm

parlors, and the one room was all white—white floor, white walls, and white ceiling. Sitting in a back seat a person felt as though he were well down in the throat of a calla lily. The red carpet on the rostrum and the ascending steps added an exotic note because no home would ever own anything so red. The three walnut and haircloth chairs with pointed backs were cherished as Gothic and the two little vases of sweet peas on the pulpit and the bowl of peonies on the table below drew the eyes toward the preacher and the organ and choir. The settees ranged in symmetrical rows. Even the horses, hitched to the fence outside, drowsed and switched their tails in the same place every Sunday. The open windows looked into an apple orchard and across green fields, rising toward the uplands or sloping toward the marshes.

The looks and dress of the congregation showed how they set the Sabbath apart. Sunday clothes joined country folk to the great world. Old gentlemen in black worsted sat beside old ladies in black silk. The local beauty wore white cashmere with pale green velvet trimmings, and her white gloves smelled of orris root; little girls snuggled together in rows of white muslin and blue sashes.

The Sunday difference in people was not only in church dress. The day showed them different facets of themselves. In rural life, neighbors near at hand could be known in all their ways, but those who lived three miles away might be known only in their sensational aspects. Mr. and Mrs. A——, soprano and baritone, were known by gossip as a couple who hardly spoke to each other at home; everything they did was for the sake of the children. In church they sang duets, "The Holy City" or "Beautiful Isle of Some-where." Those who had heard of their long compromise always held the breath a little, as if a blow might fall, between the verse and the chorus. But lightning never flashed and after awhile the music finally conveyed that the harmony was as true as the battle. The butcher was a man dreaded by children on weekdays, lest he take away the baby calf. On Sundays he had both dignity and repose. The asthma patient who could never be sure when the attack would come went to church because it calmed her; the whole history of her burden was in her suffering eyes. Withdrawn in meditation, the church-goer suggested to his fellows that everyone had more than one life.

Church was the only occasion when the hamlet saw itself all together, both sexes, all ages, the handicapped as well as the strong. Out of this time came the feeling of belonging, the willingness to cooperate, and the solidarity which wanted to protect and cherish the group.

Children were taken to church from the age of four. The rules for their deportment were as rigid as in the days of tipstaves. It was forbidden to be late, to move about, to look behind, to read or look at anything, to twist buttons or braids; indeed to do anything at all except attend to the minister and the music. No attempt was made to adapt anything to children. Their legs hung from seats well above the floor. Their minds expected not to understand much. But the child was forced into observation; he assimilated as he could.

Hardly anything, in these days, could break the tradition of composure in church. In ten years the single outcry was from a mother, standing before her child's coffin for the last look. Her screams had a frightening effect on the congregation, neighbors saying long afterward, "I can hear her still. Poor soul, she was temporarily out of her mind."

A certain rigidity in church atmosphere must have been favored by the Sunday rigidity at home. Everything dropped into slow rhythm and ordinary life and attitudes were forbidden, except about food. The mother cooked her best meals; otherwise, no unnecessary work was done. No one raised a hand; a necessary exception was tending curing hay to protect it from mildew. Formerly the forefathers had collected fines from transgressors who worked on Sunday.

Everyone bathed and dressed in his best clothes. Men shaved and loafed, but they did not gossip over the fences or go fishing. Children could not play games or with dolls or make mudpies or go to walk; if they even looked out of the window restlessly, the mother remarked, "I had to learn the Catechism and the Books of the Bible on Sunday afternoons."

The feeling of church went entirely away when the minister left. At Sunday School, there was no longer any calla lily, merely a large room. Verses, texts, the Ten Commandments, and the lesson were prepared at home on Saturday under the mother's direction. Reciting them on Sundays always missed being impressive. The laymen who took turns at being Sunday School Superintendent had an almost destructive effect. The community liked ritual but amateurs did not do ritual well.

Teaching was at least on the level of grade school teaching, but the Biblical world seemed too far away to understand. Trying to make themselves at home in it, children singing "There is a green hill far away" imagined that the cross was on one of the pasture hills, near the stone wall, while the Sea of Galilee was like the local river. Yet children always went to Sunday School. It had belonged to them from the first opening in a schoolhouse in 1817.

Prayer meetings in the church were really summer evening songfests. The cows were hustled from the pasture early Wednesday evening, so the young people could go. The older members who came opened with "Sweet Hour of Prayer" and gave testimony, always beginning with "Where two or three are gathered together." Then they encouraged the young to sing. Teen-agers, the single, and young couples sang first all the martial hymns, then all those gospel hymns which could be arranged for part singing— "Throw out the Life-line," "Let the Lower Lights be Burning," "Bringing in the Sheaves," and "Shall We Gather at the River?"

By half past eight, the whole prayer meeting was walking home together, still singing. When the crowd stopped at the spring and drank in turn from the cocoanut gourd, the tenor voice rose in the moonlight and came back from the screen of the circling trees in "When the Roll is Called Up Yonder." The place and the time produced no scoffer, but there was a professed and grieving unbeliever, a boy of eighteen with a beautiful voice. When the other boys were chanting "I'll be There," he was rumbling "I'll not be There, not, not be There."

Prayer to the young meant the prayers made in meeting and "Our Father," said every morning in school and every night before going to bed. Family prayers were not the custom; neither was grace before meat usual, except at meals where a minister chanced to be present; in that event, blessing was asked even at the church picnic. At night, small children knelt by the mother and said, "Now I lay me down to sleep," following with a long list of "God bless Papa, Mama, Johnny, Grandpa, Aunt Sarah" and so on through the relatives. One couple were said to be in perpetual duel because the mother taught the children to ask blessings on her relatives, but not on her in-laws.

Revivals used to be a powerful ally of religion. Those of

my grandparents' day—1836, 1840, and 1877—carried tor-
rential impact; in their wake, new churches were founded
and new members added to church rolls. Comparatively,
the one revival of the 1890's was a brief and mild spring
rain. The three days of meetings, including evening meetings, were crowded; they were silent, as far as the congregation was concerned, except for prayer and song, and I
cannot remember anything said about "the Wrath to
come." People who wanted to make a new start on a
Christian life or who asked for prayers stood up and the
minister came down to their seats and shook their hands.

The Camp Meeting was at times near to revival psychology. Certain meetings had the mourners' bench and
those in conflict went and knelt there. But the Board of
Directors once declined to give a second year call to a
popular Methodist preacher, on the ground that his tactics
were too sensational.

The social event of the year was the Church Picnic to
the ocean. This was a luxury; the ocean was too far away
for other days, it suggested another universe. The day was
always sunny; blue harebells grew only here; the sea
stretched on forever. The expanse of the sea cast some kind
of light on the religious mysteries.

The countryman must have felt mystery as well as anyone, but he was a silent man. He could look at the sunset
without saying anything, and he did not kiss publicly.

The preaching service was the only time he seemed accessible to mystery: "O, remember that my life is a breath
. . . Where their worm dieth not and the fire is not
quenched. . . . Buy the truth and sell it not." The minister's
voice was so magnificent that the hearer caught an il-
lumined meaning. While the voice was speaking, if for no
longer, man believed.

The church music, chiefly from Moody and Sankey's *Gospel Hymns,* was joined to the meaning of the pastor's voice. Outside of the Bible, it was the adult's only poetry, and singing it was his expression of the Unknown. Families sang hymns at home around the organ. Women sang as they made butter, little boys hunting the cattle whistled "There were ninety and nine that safely lay." Young men made up quartets in the evening and a solitary boy walking home in the dark night might be singing "Blessed Assurance."

The congregation sang very slowly, beginning with "Praise God from Whom all Blessings Flow." Harsh and thin, supported by a few boys like larks and one true soprano, the voices repeated the same hymns over and over: "My Faith Looks Up to Thee," "In the Cross of Christ I Glory," "All Hail the Power of Jesus' Name," "Sun of my Soul," "Nearer my God to Thee," "Work for the Night is Coming," "Yield not to Temptation," "What a Friend We Have in Jesus," "I Need Thee Every Hour." The variety possible in hymns was reasonably large. The music inclined to the mechanical, the words, often of self-abnegation, to the sentimental. Nevertheless, these people were not willingly articulate. Without the hymn they might never have been able to say in a lifetime, "I Surrender All."

The singing may have been planned so that every age could have a turn at finding something for its need. Young people never wanted to stop singing "Onward Christian Soldiers" and "Let the Lower Lights be Burning." It may have been the elderly who chose "How Firm a Foundation," "Blest Be the Tie that Binds" and "Safely Through Another Week."

Because the church had no winter services, the countryman did not know Christmas hymns and carols and the festival was one of family kindness rather than of religious meaning. For the same reason, Easter was not more than a name. Lent was not known, and if an adult sometimes said musingly "This is Easter," a child knew no more than the definition of the day.

Communion was a mystery on every count. It made the adults seem unfathomable to the young. The communion table covered with the finest white damask looked familiar and when the deacons lifted the cover, so did the fine old silver tankard and goblets. But the moment the ritual began, a breath came from Arctic mountains:

> 'Tis midnight and on Olive's brow
> The star is dimmed that lately shone.
> 'Tis midnight in the garden now,
> The suffering Savior prays alone.

"Take, eat, this is My Body" sounded as if it must be so, and, to children who knew the sound of waterfalls, the liquid flow of the music in "There is a Fountain Filled with Blood" gave terrible visions. The silence with the bread in the mouth, the drink from the silver goblet, and the rapt look of the communicant opened gulfs between the child and the rest of his world.

Death multiplied mystery; in winter the cold added to the inexorable in the open coffin. A grave could not be dug in the frozen ground and the only flowers would be two or three red blooms from a geranium. Yet the talk afterward showed that people felt support and comfort from the funeral service. They used to say we must learn that the end really comes, and they quoted a difficult text:

> Wherefore is light given to him that is in misery
> And life unto the bitter in soul
> Who long for death, but it cometh not.

The beliefs of the silent, inarticulate countrymen may only be speculated about. When the mother church of this area was founded, members were permitted to join "without making any public profession of their experience." This attitude of individual privacy lasted.

Memory now takes account of impalpable impressions, many of them from daily life. I think the congregation was stimulated by Biblical history but found it too far away to grasp, except through stories, parables, bits about heroes and prophets, and verses that lingered in memory. They were New Testament folk. For them the principles of Christian living were the ideal and there was a wistful appreciation of Sheldon's *In His Steps*. The need for deeds and for faith "as a grain of mustard seed" was talked about in all possible connections with life. But emphasis was on living; not on salvation. The most solemn phrases in the Lord's Prayer were "Forgive us our debts as we forgive our debtors" and "Lead us not into temptation."

The congregation loved parables, beginning with the sower who went forth to sow, and they had ways of explanation which showed that they felt the force of symbols. Everyone in town had an interpretation for the stone the builders rejected and for the householder who paid the same shilling to those who worked all day and those who worked only from the eleventh hour. This capacity to grasp symbolism was the most soaring practical power conferred on the hamlet by the church. The mystery and symbolism of love and of Nature were experienced, but not talked about in words. Only the church offered a symbolism that was widely talked about.

When the aged minister read the passages with winged words, a marvelous light of comprehension came over some of the faces. The voice communicated; it was understood. Afterward, in prayer and testimony, the symbol could be seen passing into legend. Somewhere between the stirrup and the ground of hard necessity, the rural mind acquired the ability to twist and translate Oriental imagery and thought to its own use.

It is conceivable that practice with parables made for the acceptance of miracles. The people surely believed in God. I doubt if they believed in the Devil. Perhaps Christians sifted their theology unconsciously, tending to believe in what they were attracted to and passing over what they did not grasp. No one ever heard of a literal place of fire and brimstone. Hell was a symbol. Heaven was a vision or a reality.

Although a literal Hell and Devil had gone part way out of this church, an ancient belief in penalties remained. The devout could talk about illness, accident, and misfortune as punishment from God. The arguments the Plymouth Colonists used when the Lord seemed to be chastening His people with smallpox were created over again in the hamlet every winter. Belief in punishment—the popular word was "come-uppance"—was deeply rooted in the culture.

The everyday air conveyed the conviction that man lived under an impending Fate. It was not to be expected that he would always have good fortune. Ill fortune waited. Restraint may have come in part from intimate knowledge of other lives through preceding generations. Since everyone's experience was more or less known, an encyclopedia of sickness, poverty, and misfortune stood always open. A man absorbed what Time had done to others long before it turned upon him.

If the ordinary talk of meeting the dead in the hereafter

and the rapt singing of "Shall We Gather at the River?" count, popular belief envisioned life after death. But one never knows; I asked a very old lady, a long-time member of this church, if she expected to be re-united again with her father and mother and her husband. She said, "Child, that would be a hope, but no certainty." She was born only thirty-four years after Julia Ward Howe, who so often said in her *Diary* that she expected to find again her husband and the little Sammy she lost when he was three.

The dead were talked of, along with the living, not as beloved ghosts, but as they were in life. Families were always wondering what Father or Mother would have done in today's circumstances or what the son in the churchyard would have done if he had lived to grow up. Pictures of the dead were looked at every day, sometimes at fixed times: "always before I go to bed," "before I leave the house to go anywhere and as soon as I come back."

Our nineteenth century religion was very different from the religion that first came to isolated places like ours. When Jonathan Edwards went to Northampton, Massachusetts, in the eighteenth century, it was a frontier not unlike ours. The sheep pastures extended to Mount Tom, the roads were paths for horseback travel, the forest closed in on all sides, and the river was the only way out. When he preached on the wrath of God and everlasting punishment from the text "Their foot shall slide in due time," the congregation moaned, "Oh, I am going to hell. . . . What shall I do to be saved?"

When Jonathan Fisher walked the seventy-five miles from Blue Hill to Machias to deliver an ordination sermon, he was a man who believed that man could be delivered over to Satan. He liked to begin a sermon with "My dear hearers, there is no way to escape Divine Justice at the Great Day."

The old minister explained the differences in the generations when he delivered the *Centennial Anniversary Address* at the Mother Church in 1882.* The pioneer, coming to church by boat or through the forest, was still under the influence of John Calvin. But by the beginning of his own ministry, all New England had "softened into a mild form of moderate Calvinism." The conditions of his youth were also different from those of 1882. "Strangers transiently in town and sailors in port came to the town Prayermeeting. . . . A group of lawyers attending Court in the town walked out to the hamlet to an evening prayermeeting in the schoolhouse and joined in the prayer and testimony. . . . The church still kept an Annual Fast." By the 1890's, no sailors came, the town was no longer a port, lawyers did not walk four miles to prayer meeting.

No sermon by the Reverend H. F. Harding can be found, but he left sayings. Of the church he said that "Every jarring note of discord has sunk into the eternal silence. . . . What is of God can never die." The bell of his voice rings in memory as clear as the church bell: "Jehovah is my rock and my fortress and my deliverer. . . . If thine enemy hunger, feed him; if he thirst, give him to drink. . . . Return, ye children of men."

The strength of this church was enough to make it the dominant community influence. Not much more connected with the people than a radio commentator is today, except that the building was there, it held the neighborhood together in devotion. Long after Calvinism, a con-

* Reverend H. F. Harding. *Memorial Address of the Centennial Anniversary of the Centre Street Congregational Church at Machias, 1882* (Machias, Maine: C. O. Furbush, 1884).

genial negation lingered. People still quoted such texts as "Their foot shall slide in due time." Paired with the beautiful landscape which gave an interpretation of life through the eye, the church gave mystical interpretations of birth, life, and death through the ear.

8

School

THE ONE-ROOM SCHOOL had its ways of being as modern as tomorrow. It gave no tests, no examinations, no homework, no reports, required no excuse for absence, used no marching or other devices of drill. Children might sit where they liked. They were not promoted from grade to grade annually since there were no grades, only individuals. There was no graduation; pupils merely went to school as long as they wanted to. The only school reward was being known as a good scholar.

The hamlet was divided into two school districts, upper and lower, in terms of distance, so that, counting the return home for dinner, no child would have to walk more than four miles a day. The lower district enrolled thirty pupils from ten homes. The school year of twenty weeks was arranged in two terms of ten weeks each, one from early April to about July 3, the other from September 1 to

November 15. There was no holiday except Memorial Day.

Attendance was faithful. Weather had no effect upon it, though on very rainy days lunch was brought from home. Girls were never kept away to help at home, except in a mother's illness, and boys very rarely. There was no epidemic illness in ten years.

Distribution of pupils can be estimated for convenience in terms of today's grades. About five of the thirty children were in the equivalent of Grade I, about twenty scattered in Grades II through VII, and five, older youth up to eighteen, were in Grade VIII, or taking reviews and one or two advanced subjects which varied from term to term. The schoolroom then always held three groups, the little ones, the intermediates, and the older students. Classes for the oldest and youngest were fairly fixed, intermediate work was flexible. Children shifted from class to class, reading with one group, doing arithmetic with another, and geography with a third, so that progress was individual.

The educational standards of this period can best be illustrated by their results. Two children, one twelve years old and the other fourteen, were both able to enter the eighth grade in the town schools. One had attended the hamlet school for four years and the other for eight years. The school system of the town, molded by college entrance requirements, was considered excellent.

The schoolhouse beside the road had a scenic location, facing the two rivers in the valley and looking the usual two miles to the horizon. "Around it still the sumach grows and blackberry vines are running." The children always wondered how Whittier knew exactly what grew around their schoolhouse.

Three mighty balm-of-Gilead trees shaded the unfenced

school yard. Along the roadside wonderful granite rocks and ledges stretched for two hundred feet. At recess children swarmed over them, playing house. Smooth hollowed-out rocks served for chairs and beds, flat-topped rocks for tables. Sloping ledges became castles; they had exquisite little gardens of grasses and mosses and yellow cinquefoil around the edges. The color of this granite varied from gray, sparkling with bits of mica, to black and white; an occasional quartz formation might be pearly or rosy. When a small rock split apart, a wild rose grew and blossomed in the crevice; when a large one yawned open, a silver birch rose out of a few handfuls of dirt. Close by in a field stood a very Mount Everest of a boulder; as big as a house, it defied most climbers. At the top of Schoolhouse Hill, the Looking Rock jutted in a point toward the West. On the way to school, children were oppressed with duty but on the way home they used to run to its summit to look off into the distance and feel free.

The school tax for this area began in 1790 when the assessment was £21 7ₛ. The little yellow building must have been built before the hamlet was set off in 1846; it was crowded to the doors in the 1860's and 1870's. The bulk of it was set well on the ground and the roof had a gentle slope. The broad pine floor boards, scrubbed white, had come from the adjoining pasture; the room had views and was sunny. The blue-gray desks, with their box-like seats, seated two children each. The teacher's desk and chair, symbol of a throne, stood on a platform a foot high. The walls were white, and the stove was a black sheet-iron rectangle.

The equipment consisted of two blackboards, the text books, the galvanized water pail with its long tin dipper, a wall map of North America, and black and white repro-

ductions of Watts-Dunton's "Sir Galahad" and Rosa Bon-
heur's "Pharaoh's Horses." The textbooks were free.
Parents, who had had to buy their own, were insistent about
their care. Every book was covered at home with calico
from the mother's piece bag, firmly sewn into place. Children were taught how to turn the pages and about having
clean hands and treating a book respectfully.

The girls sat on "the girls' side," the right hand side,
wearing summer ginghams or white calico pinafores over
wool frocks, their two long braids tied with hair ribbons.
They wore long black stockings and black shoes, the shoes
always scuffing against the footstools. The boys across the
aisles looked tall and slender in light blouses and tight knee
pants. Their chief ambition was to get into long trousers
and it might take a year to wear down parental resistance.
Children always wanted to go barefooted to school, and the
smaller children did so.

Most children could read when they came to school;
they knew the alphabet more or less and could spell a few
words of one syllable. The teacher never had help from
older pupils or monitors. She carried the program by hearing one class orally while another was set to writing a lesson
out on the blackboard, by constantly shifting pupils within
groups, and by tutoring older boys and girls at recess.

Attending an ungraded school where voices were always
reciting is rather like doing office work with the radio going all the time. The pupil paid no attention to classes
below his own level, just as the accustomed ear does not
hear the commercials, but he followed everything above
his level thirstily, as if it were a much more valuable message
than his own work. It was also dramatic to hear the big
boys and girls recite; a child would even learn to listen
without looking up from his book.

Children came in the morning at nine, carrying bunches of violets for the teacher and pale yellow apples from the "Old Hardy" tree. When the teacher standing in the door finished ringing her hand bell, school opened. The day's schedule and the general line of the work went like this:

9:00— 9:15......Bible Reading, Lord's Prayer, Calling the Roll
9:15— 9:30......Reading I (Arithmetic II, blackboard)
9:30—10:00......Reading II, III (Arithmetic I, blackboard)
10:00—10:30......Arithmetic III (Grammar I, blackboard)
10:30—10:45......*Recess* (Tutoring older pupils in Grammar)
10:45—11:15......Geography II (Geography I, blackboard)
11:15—11:45......History I
11:45—12:00......Hygiene

1:30— 1:45......Hymn Singing
1:45— 2:15......Writing (Monday and Wednesday); Advanced Reading (Tuesday, Thursday and Friday)
2:15— 2:35......History II (Arithmetic or Grammar, blackboard)
2:35— 2:45......Reading I
2:45— 3:00......*Recess* (Tutoring older pupils in Arithmetic)
3:00— 3:30......Advanced Arithmetic and Algebra
3:30— 4:00......Spelling

The school day began with the teacher reading a chapter from the Bible, usually from the Psalms or the New Testament, and then everyone bowed the head and repeated the Lord's Prayer. Religious observances were then customary in schools all over the area. Instead of the Scripture reading, Psalm XXIII or CIII was sometimes repeated in unison by all the children. Choral speaking was a residue of church and Sunday School; no one ever committed either verses or hymns to memory at school.

The hymns sung at the opening of school in the afternoon constituted the extent of the child's self-expression. Taking turns, each pupil chose the music about twice a term. The privilege was cherished as if the unaccompanied voices were a great orchestra; a girl would announce weeks ahead the hymn she intended to select. Hymns were sung with gusto, everyone was rosy and hearty, fresh from a meal and a walk; but the favorite hymn of one of the algebra students was:

> Rescue the perishing, care for the dying,
> Snatch them in pity from sin and the grave.

The most important subjects in the course of study were arithmetic, spelling, and grammar, in this order. Spare time went to reviewing, perfecting accuracy, with all of the students participating to improve their knowledge of these subjects.

Small children stood on benches fastened to the wall and worked the examples—addition, subtraction, multiplication and division—ready for them on the blackboard while, out of the corner of her eye, the teacher observed them as she taught another class. A pupil began to write the "two's table" and had to go on and on and on until at last he was able to write the "twelves" backward.

Later, emphasis moved to the cost of plastering houses, painting and papering rooms, and the like, though always without experience in measuring walls or reference to familiar rooms. Problems in percentage were usually taught in terms of money; children only found out for themselves that percentage could be done with apples. Square root was taught with intensity and was actually a popular topic.

Language study was divided into content and structure. For content, there was a graded series of five *Readers*. Pupils read aloud in turn and were corrected for accent, pronunciation, and emphasis. Memorizing was not required, but many children could repeat snatches of Celia Thaxter, "Crossing the Bar," and parts of "The Vision of Sir Launfal."

The preference was for poetry and for subjects of war, love, and death. A story about Beethoven's deafness and his *Sonata in F* was much loved and so was the account of Lincoln's reprieve of the young soldier who slept on guard duty. "Mrs. Caudle's Umbrella Lecture" was enjoyed as hilariously funny and it used to be said that Mrs. Caudle's voice must sound exactly like that of an unpopular local woman. The school had no paper-bound classics; the *Readers* were the only reading material.

The most worn and battered book was the *Speller*. All grades used the same spelling book and everyone knew that his spelling would be held to strict account. *Spellers* always came to hand as soon as other work was in control. The prose in the *Speller* was divided between reprints about Nature, quotations, and historical writing. One page would be built on "Washington's Farewell Address," the next would be poetry:

> The snow had begun in the gloaming
> And busily all the night
> Had been heaping field and highway
> With a silence deep and white.

Pupils would be held responsible for spelling any words in the prose, then for long lists of words, including many no one would ever use or hear, and finally for confusing words, such as *believe, receive, offense, defense.*

Friday was the most exciting school day because, at about three o'clock in the afternoon, there was a long spelling match in which everyone took part. The teacher appointed the two captains who chose alternately for their sides, trying to get the best spellers, until all were standing in two rows facing each other. Small children loved the match, because they were tested only on words within their experience. No one ever wanted to sit down, but as fast as they missed a word, the spellers had to take their seats. The ideal was for the two captains to survive the longest and to spell against each other for some time, conquered in the end only by the deliberate use of tricky and difficult words. The winner was regarded as home-run heroes are today, and the whole match was lived over again around home supper tables.

Grammar, on the other hand, was almost always a written exercise. It was taught almost as if it were a translation from a foreign language. The beginner must first be able to repeat the formal definitions of the parts of speech, the kinds of sentences and moods. The chief aim of grammar lessons was for the pupil to be good enough to stand at the blackboard and analyze prose indefinitely, making a diagram. He made a box over every word and wrote in the part of speech, showing modifiers and word relationships with slanting lines until a distinctive skeletal structure emerged.

Original compositions or even letters were not required. The reason written lessons were limited to the blackboard may have been that the teachers wanted to spare themselves the correction of papers or slates. Handwriting was taught by imitating the copy in *Writing Books*, which said "Practice makes perfect" or "Speech is silver but silence is golden."

Geography was taught from Frye's *Geography*, one small book of text and one of atlas size. It was a drill subject to be memorized, an extension of the point of view and methods used in spelling and grammar. The teacher used to say easily, "Next time, take the next ten pages" or "Take China." The schoolroom echoed to the definitions of continent, island, peninsula, cape, and isthmus, to the "bounding" of foreign countries, and the naming of their rivers, mountains, cities, and products. When study reached their native state, the children learned to singsong the names of all the counties with their rivers and shire towns. Maps were traced first for practice, then done freehand upon slates and blackboards.

The history text was Bancroft's *History of the United States*. Since there was but one book and the tendency of all teachers was to start at the beginning every term, the Colonial period became a tale many times told and it was almost impossible to get beyond the Civil War. It was a hindrance inherent in the short, separated school terms that most children were always at the beginning of every book, year after year. Eager readers applied themselves to racing through all their books as soon as they got them. After that, there was never any more surprise. The others might grow in years and even in interests of the mind without ever finding out what was in the last quarter of their texts.

Children thought that nothing much ever happened after colonization except wars. The French and Indian War was no sooner ended than the Revolution began and telescoped itself into the Civil War. The mild and kindly women who taught the schools had a desperate need to rely on men's courage, for they exacted again and again the dates of battles, the commanders, and the winners. Children with good visual memories could repeat Bancroft on the Battle of Gettysburg for four or five pages, as if they were reading from the book: "First Day . . . Second Day . . . Third Day . . ." Afterward, on the playground, they used to stamp around singing, "Sherman's dashing Yankee boys are marching to the coast." Terrible ideas about winning were probably put into children's minds, for the loser was always wrong and viewed with happy contempt.

Industrialization was only a topic to recite upon; no one understood that it had touched the hamlet. The Westward Movement was passed over in the same way, although migrants from houses near the schoolhouse had traveled with the '49ers.

Invention was different; it drew a delighted attention. The sewing machine, the locomotive, and the steamboat were favorite inventions and one household had a model of the Monitor, used for war games in the brook. The cotton gin was a mystery; even the growing of cotton could hardly be imagined. An odd fillip of interest was added to the cotton gin because the hamlet had a deserted farm called "the Jim Whitney place." Lilacs grew out of the cellar hole and the fields had hawthorns, apple trees, and currants in little patches. Children used to pretend that this farm was someway related to Eli Whitney; he had perhaps been there on a visit.

The text on *Hygiene*, small and new, must have been the result of someone's theory of keeping up with the times. Usually it was only read aloud, though the readers had to learn lists of the bones and the circulation of the blood "by heart." No one noticed that the author was a bit rabid on the evils of tobacco and alcohol, but children began to say that they did not believe some of their parents' ideas about digestion or that one must always eat bread along with jam, "then it won't hurt you."

The practical application of hygiene in the school now appears shocking. Some children were told at home never to take a drink of water at school, no matter how thirsty they were. The spring drinking water was kept in an open pail, with only one dipper. No provision was made for washing the hands. Girls used to walk down the road to the horse watering trough and hold their hands under the pipe sometimes, but boys merely left washing alone. The privy at the back of the schoolhouse was cared for according to the standards of the day, except that it was necessary to carry one's own toilet paper. In the schoolroom, someone was always spitting on a slate. Pupils used slates all day long, wrote and rubbed out their writing. Girls brought an old cologne bottle from home, kept it filled with water, and used a sponge or slate-rag for this erasing; boys just spit.

The curriculum was kept absolutely separate and far away from the locale, almost as if things were better that way. Morals, cleanliness, and manners were not in the school's province, any more than if it had been a university. Local history could be learned at home. Mary's grandmother could tell all about the two Weston girls who carried powder and bullet material through the woods in the Revolution; one of them had been her grandmother and she had heard it from her. In school one must commit to memory the battles one had never heard of. Examples of an island or a cape given in the geography class had better be Madagascar or the Cape of Good Hope, even if the pond back of the schoolhouse had a little island in the center and a cape at one point.

Inaccuracy about names was a grievous handicap to

learning with exactness. Middle River was called "the
River," Pumpkin Ridge was "the hills," any variety of a
sparrow was simply a sparrow, daisies were "white weed,"
mushrooms were "toadstools," butterflies, moths, and in-
sects, barely noticed, were called "bugs." To be known,
an insect had to bite or sting. The only exceptions to this
indifference were the many women who knew a good deal
about flowers, shrubs, and barks.

The teachers—four women and one man in six years—
were people of character and of adequate education in subject matter. One had gone only to country school and
some Teachers' Institutes; one had graduated from Normal
School, and the others were high school graduates. All of
them seemed fearfully old to children, but they were really
from twenty-five to forty-five or thereabouts. They knew
how to organize the day to get everything in, but had almost no ability to relate anything to a child's experience.
Parents undoubtedly supported this position, the elders pre-
ferring that learning be as abstract as possible. Neighboring
schools might teach the names of birds; in our hamlet it
was counted worse than foolishness.

Parents used to say that when they went to this school
after the Civil War, there had been more than twice as
many children. They had carried their McGuffey's *Reader*
back and forth and some had used inherited copies of Noah
Webster's *Speller*. They had *Arithmetics,* but no history,
geography, or hygiene books; no tablets and pencils, only
slates. They could still spell, parse sentences, and do mental
arithmetic better than their children.

Mother visited school on the Last Day to hear Caroline
recite "Curfew Shall Not Ring Tonight," and to talk with
other mothers as they ate pink marshmallow candy and
bananas. Fathers never went near; visiting school would

have been effeminate. At home parents talked freely about the teacher. There were two tests of a good teacher: if she kept good order, and if she could work any example in the *Arithmetic* at once and correctly. A teacher who wanted to emphasize anything outside of arithmetic must be covering up ignorance of the fundamentals.

The neighborhood preferred a single woman as teacher, reasoning that her school work would be her main interest. The man who taught a year was judged lacking in understanding of small children. The married woman's salary of $30 a month was resented—"Let her husband take care of her." One of the teachers was regarded as "too tony," meaning highbrow. Her home in the town was so distinguished and her diction so Bostonian that people thought she must feel herself too good for the country. Another teacher was a Roman Catholic and was looked on as an alien in a Protestant group. Home talk about Catholics echoed the class system of the town, where some of the Irish Catholics lived in poor neighborhoods.

Parents were always saying casually that a punishment at school would mean a second one at home. There was no unruly behavior, no corporal punishment, and the students had no idea of plaguing the teacher. Tardiness was a sin which met instant public reproof. Boys who threw spitballs or chewed gum might have to stand in the middle of the floor for punishment. Slow learners might be kept in at recess to study, but disapproval was the most usual discipline.

Incentives to good conduct were hardly needed, but there was a system of awarding little pink pasteboards marked MERIT at the end of the day. A dozen of these MERITS could be exchanged for a highly calendered landscape or flower picture about five by seven inches. Choosing the picture card was enjoyable; they were kept in an old stationery box, as the start of a "collection." At the same time, it was customary to be a little chilly about the pink tickets; only the smallest children wanted them.

The teacher never came to the playground, but a good many games had been learned somehow: baseball was played as much as possible, girls playing only with girls; running and singing games like London Bridge, Drop the Handkerchief, Blind Man's Bluff, Puss in a Corner, and A Tiskit, a Tasket were popular. When it was too warm for running, the older girls walked off with their arms around each other, the small girls played on the ledges, and the boys assembled by the side of the schoolhouse to tell tall stories. When it became known all over the hamlet that a boy had "the bad disease" (gonorrhea), it was because he boasted of it to the boys' group at recess.

When children played at home, they did not use the school games, but made up stories and acted them. A little circle of seven—four girls and three boys—were inseparable in playtime from about the eighth to the eleventh year. They played house in the old organ box, taking turns in being father, mother, child, and guests; they had a tricycle and used it for games about horses. The plays they made up were embroidered from scraps someone had read: Indians, hunters, explorers, the life of Buffalo Bill, The Midnight Ride of Paul Revere—the rider brandishing the family lantern—the death of De Soto, and the parable of the Prodigal Son.

Games were only one of several subjects learned outside the school curriculum; other new learning was about social class, sex, and personality.

The first instruction about social class in the hamlet came from the mothers. When the child was well started in school he was told that at school one played with everyone but on leaving school one played only with one's own friends. This was because some families were lazy, or gossiped, or had some invisible stain from some ancestor long ago. The houses of such families were not to be entered; their dooryards were not even to be stepped into. The children who lived there were not to blame, but sooner or later they would be like the rest of the family. These warnings were received with bewilderment and protests. It was not possible to believe in such a classification, but the idea that classifications existed was planted.

There are no data which show when sex awareness began in young children: it appeared to arise from the older boys' and girls' interest in it. Romance was almost forced on nine-year-olds because of a dementia of writing down boys' and girls' names in pairs, then crossing out all the matching letters, and counting those left—as one pulled daisy petals— saying "Friendship, Love, Courtship, Marriage." A small child did not care who went with whom but could get fascinated crossing out the letters and enumerating:

MARIE ELEANOR HAYES
ROY LAMAN MORRIN
LOVE

Girls used to experiment with crossing out their parents' names, and then as a great idea, George Washington and Martha Custis, Abraham Lincoln and Mary Todd. If the names of some couple married for years came out "Friendship," it merely meant "Of course they're friends."

Pine walls took pencil well. The school woodshed and the two privies had many of these names written in pairs. Sometimes the names were cut with a jack-knife within an incised heart. Crude ellipses meant as the genitals were also cut into the walls. They were very literal, and never as varied as the sexual symbols of primitive peoples.

Girls were offended when anyone except themselves went into their privy. Any acquaintance's name written on their wall was at once blacked out. Still, some of these markings had been on the wall for a long time; conceivably passers-by may have done some of the writing in the un-locked buildings. The girls' attention seemed to fade except when new names were added. A taboo that the building should not be used by both sexes at the same time was al-ways kept.

The sexual carvings must have been the seed of the girls' Secret Society, generally called "S.S." Its badge was a bow of pink ribbon and its object was to find out how babies came. Members, sitting on the tops of the biggest rocks at recess, had no trouble finding a "secret" to tell every day as was the requirement, but they were soon unable to cor-relate their information or to agree upon the interpretation of it.

The functions of the bull, the stallion, and the rooster were always known vaguely by farm children. It was known that hens' eggs would not hatch chickens without male fertilization. The child, however, thought of these matings as part of the animal world. His world was "higher"; it did not occur to him to make comparisons. The S.S. finally agreed that babies came through the navel; probably it just opened when the time came. After that, the project lost motive and, behaving as adult research projects sometimes do, it dwindled away.

The idea of personality came through the Superintendent of Schools. He was the hamlet's prototype of the learned man. He looked like a Dickens' character, with a dash of

Irish; he had flying plumes of white hair, a long white beard, fine teeth, and piercing grey eyes. He must have been nearing eighty when he gave up his school office.

When he visited classes, he sat with clasped hands looking straight at whomever was reciting. His smile, his sparkle, and his attention would draw a child suddenly into communication with him. Parents and teachers when they heard lessons had some look of tension; this man had not, he was listening and being happy.

If a child were attracted to books, the old man kept holding out the rewards of getting to Latin. After the traveler had reached Latin, he said, "Now, just one year more and you'll be ready for the Greek." He used to talk about Carlyle and he rolled off quotations from Shakespeare and Milton. The audience did not realize until half a lifetime afterward that he did not mean merely blindness when he said, "When I consider how my light is spent. . . ."

His neighbors could hardly have known what the School Superintendent was talking about, but perhaps he brought his learning out only for the young. Parents admired him and children liked to call upon him at his home on summer afternoons. He would advise the boys about their future and urge the girls to take more schooling. His wife would bring out a plate of gingerbread, and she used to tell the aged mother in the corner to which families the callers belonged. When it was time to go, he walked in the garden with the children and picked bouquets of spicy old-fashioned pinks for the girls.

School was more interesting than some of the chores the farm exacted and children missed it when it was over. In general they liked school. Girls might have frightful dreams about arithmetic and boys might wish to avoid so much grammar, but still school created excitement.

The emphasis on verbal memory made for people who were sure of themselves. Once learned by heart, everything in the books seemed true. Knowledge was made to seem a lofty reality, vast, remote, impersonal, yet priceless. The one-room school conveyed a feeling that learning was better than other things.

9

Pleasure and Renewal

NATIONAL STUDIES of pleasure and renewal today begin with the aura of travel, vacation, week-ends, holidays, reading, music, movies, television, speed, number to be killed in traffic, costs, getting away from home.

In the long-ago hamlet, man's greater renewals came out of work, weather, seasons, school and church, personal relations, and surroundings. A person had only to be still and let them come. Outside of work, the countryman lived almost as quietly as trees through the seasons, rain, drought, wind, snowbanks, leaf, flower, fruit, bare boughs. His minor recreations lay in the rhythms of eating, sleeping, toil, and rest, and in his holidays and entertainments. Some of them were not very different from what English towns had in 1800.

The year's calendar had five legal holidays: New Year's, Memorial Day, July Fourth, Thanksgiving, and Christmas. When the chief events and holidays are listed in their seasonal movement, work and play overlap. Harvesting is farm work, but the delights of it are more than those of winter sports. Summer vacations were only the length of a day between morning and evening milking. Saturday was like any other day, no special thought was given to the week-end.

The year seemed to begin in mid-April with Town Meeting; soon after that came the Arbutus Walk, trout fishing, the opening of school, Arbor Day, May Day, more travel on the roads. During July and August, church, Sunday School, and prayer meeting returned, and there were strawberrying, swimming, the Pondlily Walk, blueberrying, raspberrying, blackberrying, the church Picnic, the Circus, and Camp Meeting. Itinerant peddlers, Indians, and summer visitors went by every day.

In September and October, the County Fair lasted a week, the herb gathering, cranberry and hop picking, apple gathering, and, with cool weather, hog killing, went on until real cold settled in. Winter lasted from November to April, with hunting, coasting, skating, spelling bees, dancing school, calls, visiting and, in the house, reading, games, music, and needlecraft. The roads grew silent and stretched into white space.

Summer amusements were more or less solitary or within the family. Winter pleasures were in part the sociability of groups, but almost nothing was organized formally. The Ladies' Aid Society was the only social organization in the community. It was a group of the older women sewing and quilting to make money for the church, sometimes having church dinners. Three couples belonged to the Grange in town and two men to the International Order of Foresters.

Children in red hoods and mittens spent their free time from before Thanksgiving to April dragging a sled up a hill and skimming down on the crust. Young people coasted by full moon when breath showed in the cold air, beginning in the dooryard and rushing across the fields to the pines in the lower pasture. Sliding when the night was bright as day was like being joined to the sky.

Pastures had oval ponds where the skater's flying scarf touched the tips of the fir boughs as he circled the edge. Sleigh riding, under fur robes in a flurry of bells and sprinkling snow, called with splendor to adolescents just learning to drive and was the peak of living to courting couples. Children and older people cared less about sleighing. Women who had come to the age of hoods and shawls said that they only rode to get somewhere.

The height of winter gaiety was the parties for young people. A boy rode around on horseback and said, "Father and Mother want you to come over Friday night to a party." When the guest arrived, about seven o'clock, the first floor of the house lay in a warm open circle with fires in every room. The crowd stood around the organ singing "There is a Tavern in the Town." Beginning at the first page of *Popular Song Classics*, the organist played every tune anyone called for, with repeats of "Juanita" and all the Stephen Foster songs. When games began, "Going to Jerusalem" started a screaming rough-house which continued with "Spin the Cover." "Forfeits" amused for some time if the referee invented clever penalties:

> Heavy, heavy hangs over thy head—
> What shall the owner do to redeem it?
>
> Fine or Superfine?

Superfine.

> She shall kneel to the wittiest,
> Bow to the prettiest
> And kiss the one that she loves best.

The players made mirth by being hesitant and truthful. Friends were reluctant to kiss one person, lest another be slighted. A girl who had two brothers would flush with confusion as soon as she had bowed and knelt. She did not want to tell which brother she loved best.

The games had an English flavor and parents had played them in their time. The favorite was "The Needle's Eye." It ran in a song and dance rhythm and sooner or later involved every couple in a ritual which demanded that the girl either kiss or turn the cheek. A couple standing on two chairs held hands high over the heads of the players who marched in a swinging circle through all the rooms, holding hands and singing:

> The Needle's eye it is so fine;
> The thread it runs so true.
> I have met many a smiling lass
> And now I have met you.

> (Chorus)

> Oh, she dresses neat
> And she kisses sweet.
> We do intend
> Before we end
> To see this couple meet.

Solos varied the game and at the moment when the couple dropped their hands on another boy and girl as successors, they kissed; that is to say, the boy kissed, perhaps the tip of an ear. The girl's lack of cooperation was no barrier; other boys who thought she might kiss them chose her eagerly. This game used to be played over and over through an incredible number of verses.

Another kissing game, "Postoffice," was good for only a few minutes. The two who participated went into a darkened room to exchange "a letter, a post card, or a telegram." The others waiting, hoping for squeals, soon became bored.

For these parties the hosts provided mountains of chocolate, cocoanut and marble cakes, coffee, and for those who did not drink coffee, lemonade or raspberry shrub. After awhile, the players sat in a circle eating and looking at each other, the girls in high pompadours and huge hair-ribbons above bright silk blouses, the boys in their Sunday navy blues.

By eleven o'clock, everyone was on the way home. Pairing off carried meaning. "May I see you home?" was the proof of the girl's charm. A boy who was refused lost social standing. Who went home with whom was part of the verbal gossip column, but the code required that no couple leave the group. The whole crowd walked together and conversation had to be general until the lane turned off to the girl's house.

Spelling bees were an exercise of memory, like an "Information Please" program. They drew the whole neighborhood back to the schoolhouse. Grown-ups and teenagers spelled together and an adroit manager could spin out a long evening of general participation and applause before the battle between the best spellers. These evenings made for agreeable excitement; reputations were being made. Parents who had been out of school a long time sometimes outlasted the best of the young. Real drama struck when two neighbors who did not speak to each other were opposed, or when a mother "spelled down" her sixteen-year-old daughter.

Dancing School was held in the schoolhouse one evening a week for a series, sometimes at the edge of fall or spring, so the weather would not be too cold. The young men arranged everything and each invited a young woman. If young women were scarce, a youth might call trembling on the parents of a girl of fifteen or sixteen, to ask if he might escort her. The parents would decline and the girl might not even know it until long afterward. When the hamlet was isolated, Dancing School was considered obligatory as a place of manners and polish. By the 1890's it was frowned on, because rowdy boys from neighboring hamlets used to invade without being asked, showing off to the girls and offering the boys drinks from bottles of Jamaica ginger.

Singing School was a serious undertaking of earlier years which had ended before this period. Its textbook, *Church Chorals and Choir Studies,** was still around in some homes. Both the words and the music were better than the religious music popular in 1900.

Recreation functioned chiefly in terms of the young and of whole families. After marriage, newly-weds became stay-at-homes or went around with older people.

The winter need to escape brought long calls on the neighbors in both afternoon and evening. Families sitting around the kitchen lamp used to like to hear the snow crunch on the walk on winter nights. Neighbors they had not seen since the County Fair had walked over to spend the evening. Three hours of talk could range well over the community and the town; there was never much over national issues except the presidency, nothing international

---

* R. Storrs Willis, *Church Chorals and Choir Studies* (New York: Austin & Smith, 1850).

except the Dreyfus case. The mother made coffee and cut a cake, and the children went down cellar and brought up a pan full of Baldwin apples.

Afternoon callers dropped in often. Men came to play checkers, and women came, bundled in shawls and fascinators, carrying knitting or mending. Girls came carrying their crocheting or workbags of the silk pieces they were making into a quilt; children came to play dolls. Children often went to spend the afternoon with favorite adults, handling all the treasures in the button box, sewing on the little toy machine that took the cloth into a bird's beak, and trying on costumes of long ago. Food was always brought out, but children did not rate cake or pie; they got along on cookies, apples, or scraped turnips.

The winter evenings began at six o'clock, and were so long that games were a necessity. Families played geography games, mental arithmetic, checkers, *Lotto, Old Maid*, and *Authors* night after night. The *Authors* cards had pictures of the writers and lists of their works. People who had never read a word of Dickens or George Eliot knew what they looked like and the names of half a dozen of their novels.

Local opinion was against card playing—"I wouldn't have a deck of cards in the house." People liked to say that they were "not Methodists," did not think cards wicked and could take them or leave them. The theory was that one should not indulge in mere time-killing or foster an amusement which sometimes led to bad associations.

In a way hard to explain, women's disapproval of cards may have been reaction against the many women's card clubs of "The 400" in town. The newspaper carried weekly stories about these clubs, the participants, the refreshments, decorations, and guests of honor. A vision of an exclusiveness to which farm women were not eligible was thus open. It could not but be a slur; and if the hostess had ever tried to bargain too sharply for farm produce or to put her household help into the servant class, her whist party could be resented years afterward.

Saint Valentine's Day meant a lift to the young, because it was their day and the only flash of festival spirit in a long interval of cold. Girls saved gold, silver, and lace paper all winter to make valentines for their best friends. No names were signed to valentines, because guessing was part of the rules. The best auspices for the evening of February 14 were black darkness. Messengers were going to tiptoe to doors, give a big knock, then run away, giggling and panting.

The male part of this celebration—unless a boy were old enough to buy a missive for a girl—was to buy dreadful comics for all the adults they had a grudge against. Comic valentines were broadsides on cheap paper, with ugly pictures and hateful rhymes; they taunted misers, hypocrites, Old Maids, and faults of temperament. Because they were printed, and being in print made it so, the jibes were puzzled over for a long time. They hurt the feelings of whole families.

Everyone owned from hundreds to thousands of trees, yet there was still the wish to plant trees on Arbor Day. A father would buy and set out a cherry tree for each of his three children; "Grace," "Caroline," and "William"— each tree was given a child's name. A mother would have a mountain ash or a tamarack transplanted, Boston apple trees would be set out, and more balm-of-Gileads would join the windbreak at the roadside.

The May festivals bloomed with flowers. On the first of May children traveled around in the evening, hanging May-baskets. Long winter afternoons went into the making of these baskets out of cardboard and tissue paper. Round, square, oval, diamond-pointed, hat-shaped, they were covered with fringed tissue in palest pink, white, peach, and yellow, filled with mosses and tiny artificial flowers. To find a Maybasket on the doorstep was like the moment of opening a florist's box.

On a May Sunday, bands of young men walked back into the forest after trailing arbutus. The Arbutus Walk had some of the elements of mystery, as if the elect could scale Mount Fuji and others could only wait around at the foot. The mayflowers were distant, fragile, rare. The search was long, arduous, male. No woman ever knew the ground where they grew. When the boys came back at night, they tied up little nosegays of pale mayflowers among tough green leaves and distributed them to girls and women all over the settlement.

The young men's summer walk for pondlilies followed the same; distance, maleness, a secret place. The pearly white flowers with the quivering yellow stamens and the pink streaks on the calyx were longed for, perhaps as a contrast to the neat elegance of dooryard flowers. The starry profusion of them spattering some inland lake was imagined with intensity. A girl of marrying age thrust her pondlily carelessly in her hair but the elderly kept theirs alive tenderly, changing the water every day. The arbutus and the pondlily were the only flowers men brought publicly to women. It remains lovable that they brought them to all women, house by house.

Memorial Day was as important as Thanksgiving and Christmas. The Civil War had been ours and the Revolutionary great-grandparents in the cemetery were ours. Nothing availed against Death; there remained only mourning and remembrance. The morning ceremony was held in the church, presided over by three old Civil War veterans in blue, with brass buttons and campaign hats.

All of them were considerably damaged. The one on crutches had lost a leg and wore his trousers' leg pinned up. The one who could not turn his head had a bullet in him from Gettysburg. The third had been a prisoner in Andersonville. What they said was repetitious but their bodies had eloquence and as they told war stories their eyes flashed the courage and glory of Man.

In between the veteran's speeches, girls used to recite "The Blue and the Gray," and boys the "Gettysburg Address." Everyone sang "The Battle Hymn of the Republic" and "Tenting on the Old Camp Ground." After the benediction, veterans, teachers, parents, and children straggled into line behind the flag and walked, carrying the flowers, up the long hill to the cemetery.

At home at dinner, the elders talked about the brothers, aunts, and grandparents who had "gone before." Children started on another long walk to take flowers to the little private burying grounds in the fields. In an average spring the bouquets were apple blossoms; in a late season, they had to be the blossoming boughs of the wild pear tree. A child alone, going to sleep that night would repeat to himself:

> On Fame's eternal camping grounds,
> Their silent tents are spread,
> And Glory guards with solemn round. . . .

The church which gave the young the first ideas of how men surpass themselves, also managed the only community gathering for having fun: the picnic at the ocean, eight miles away. The hayrack ride for children, cuddled in the hay and singing, was as fine as going in a chariot. At

Roque Bluffs, harebells grew to the very cliff edge, and lupine by the roadside. Pebbles on the beach were rubbed smooth as eggs. The wind swept cold off the sea. The waters swayed toward a far horizon; probably they really did reach to Spain. The fathers steamed clams and cooked lobsters and the mothers put a big spread on white table-cloths on the sand. The pleasure was all in the strangeness. No boats and no bathing, but it was astonishing to watch adults at play and see how different they were from every day.

Picnics were not entered into lightly; they were too much work for a mere family affair. The Last-Day-of-School Picnic was managed by the teachers; children swung too high, played games too long, ate too much, and walked home very tired.

July Fourth was a gala day, with memories dipped from the Revolution which had begun down the bay. The fire-crackers were all used up in the early morning and then nothing remained but waiting for the Calithumpian Parade. Boys dressed as Indians, soldiers, highwaymen, and clowns, masked if possible, rode on their horses into every door-yard. The dinner traditional to the day was new peas and new potatoes, the first of the year from the garden, with wild strawberries smothered in yellow cream and hot bis-cuits to follow. Meat would be too much to expect unless a chicken were ready for the pot, but everyone who felt the need of something more substantial could always have stripped fish.

Once in a while the Ladies Aid Society served a chicken dinner on the Fourth; plates of ice cream sold at five cents all the afternoon. In the evening, families drove to town to the Band Concert in the Square. All the players could be identified: the leader with the baton was the druggist; the drummer was Mr. A—— who fitted one's shoes; the grocer played the drum. The horses cavorted at Sousa's marches, and the spray in the fountain was set higher than usual. Children became more anti-British than ever after Independence Day. All the masks and music and leisure were because Americans were so glad to have gotten away from the Crown. The Liberty Pole had been near the site of the town bandstand.

Summer was the time of joy. Something new—a person, a flower, a fruit, the tallyho's bugle—turned up every day. The clover fields dried from pink and red blooms to new-mown hay; all day wild roses perfumed the roadside and white ones the garden, and honeysuckle all the evening.

In warm weather, people got acquainted with the domestic animals which in winter were mainly responsibilities to feed, take care of, and keep warm. Horses were known by name as "Elden Brown's 'Phenomenon' " or "the Jones' 'Maid F.' " One horse named Dixie had once been around the track in about two minutes; he had reputation.

A horse used to be the first thing a baby was afraid of. Later on children identified themselves with horses and when adults were more than usually unfeeling would run and cling to the horse's legs and burrow in his side. After they read *Black Beauty*, they made up long stories in which they were Black Beauty or Ginger.

Cows were named elaborately—"Buttercup," "Clover," "Sweetmeat," "Barbados"—but somehow cows were always a little disliked for being obstinate. If they wanted to stay out on a warm night, they knew better than to let their bells ring.

Every cat had a name and sometimes roosters and hens had names. When the farm had new foals, calves, pigs, and kittens, women and children gave them human thoughts and feelings. Animals were either ignored or personified.

For people who owned domestic animals and lived next door to a tradition of wild ones, the Circus which camped on the Fairground for three or four days was the most exotic pleasure of the year. It translated the known into just enough of the unknown. The lions, tigers, elephants, and giraffes passed from the pictures in the Geography into life. To go to the Circus once was to keep on thinking about it until it came again. These wild animals could in fancy leap and skulk among the pines and along the ledges. The snakes were just as they had been imagined, as real as in Bible days. Horseback riding, the Parade, tumbling, and music were marvelous. The Fat Lady, the Tattooed Man, and even the clowns, were regarded as faintly repulsive; they seemed cruel to country instincts.

Wandering basket sellers from the Indian Reservation stopped once a year, upsetting households for an afternoon. Passamaquoddy Indians wore ordinary clothes and had always been a peaceable tribe. Their dyed sweetgrass baskets were strong and beautiful and had a delicious fragrance. But still their faces looked just like the Indian faces in Custer's last stand. At the very sight of them, thoughts about torture and scalps at the belt leaped into the mind. Women locked the doors and went down cellar with all the children. There they watched uneasily from a tiny cellar window, obscured from the outside by flowers, until the Indian with his bright load went off down the path.

Yankee peddlers driving little carts with shelves of cloth, thread, tin ware, scissors, notions, and handkerchiefs were a summer diversion. Peddlers were different from farmers. They inclined to be fast talkers, with big charms hanging from watchchains, and they drew on a fund of stories and wore the nimbus of traveled men. If the father were at home, the peddler might be asked to dinner, a familiarity possible only because his town was known, he drove through annually, and he was entertaining. After the meal, he gave some new towels to the hostess. Only the lowest economic group would have kept the peddler all night; he had to arrange an itinerary that would let him sleep in a town hotel or boarding-house.

The rag-man was on a lower social rung. He was vaguely dark, a foreigner from no-one-knew-where; he was never offered hospitality. He was greedy over the rag-bag which hung in the wood shed, a huge calico bag stuffed with all the worn out clothes not good enough for rug-making. He took the year's rags and paid in two tin dippers.

Swimming was a Sunday recreation for men only, perhaps because there was no really good place to swim along the river's marshy edge. Women never learned; it was said that they would never need to swim, and, besides it would make them less feminine.

The biggest summer event was Camp Meeting. As the only chance in a year to hear preaching and music on a large scale and worship among hundreds instead of with a few, it was the summit of religious observance. The time—late August—came in the period of relaxation after haying. Town folk left this meeting to the countrymen of the area. Families who took no other holiday sometimes built cottages on the Camp Ground and moved there for a fortnight. In the center of a leafy grove the tabernacle stood, roofed, but without walls. Around it a row of cottages painted pink, red, green, lavender, yellow—all the colors never used at home—formed a circle. A second circle of cottages surrounded the first and, beyond, the third and fourth circles ended in trees. A young minister once earned enmity by calling these circles "Vanity Fair." Up near the entrance, a comfortable rustic hotel served hearty meals. Three single women from the hamlet owned a yellow cottage together and welcomed all their friends. Others ate and rested by their own wagons. Even men who never went to church took their families, gossiped, ate, and went to meeting.

Camp Meeting was a religious gathering, so children were not allowed to treat it as amusement. They might walk down to see the lake but might not linger or go out in boats. When not at meeting, they promenaded around and around the circles of cottages, eating peanuts and trying to get away from the boredom of listening to adult conversation with strangers.

The County Fair at the Fairground by the river was the last community gathering before the winter funerals. The long barn-like buildings displayed farm exhibitions, a merry-go-round whirled to music, there were bicycle and horse races. Women showed flowers, bread, cakes, pies, pickles, preserves, jellies, quilts, rugs, garments, and poultry. Men showed fruits and vegetables, pigs, calves, cattle, and horses.

The Fair was also for country people rather than townspeople; it was informal and was for a good time and technical interests. Nothing much was for sale except candy and peanuts; people brought their food from home. Speeches and educational devices were at a minimum. The products were examined minutely by rivals and by the judges. Winning red or blue ribbons and a little money and having one's name listed in the newspaper was an honor. People enjoyed the Fair so much that they sometimes went back for another day.

The first balloon ascension of the area was from the Fairground. Floating in the air then seemed a conquering of space and the laws of gravitation. The prospect excited as much talk as the launching of the man-made Earth Satellite does now. The balloonist must be a man of desperate courage; suppose he landed in the water—there were two rivers and the bay, not to mention the ocean. The best place to watch would be up on the hills, where the view was large. Actually, the man floated across the main river and landed in a forest clearing.

After September, as the leaves fell, the landscape grew dun and the year began to draw in. Then came hog-killing time, the bright cold October morning that began a period of frenzied plenty. Summer vegetarianism ended in a meat feast, every home prodigal with food and extravagant in giving. A butcher came to do the killing, but after that every family knew how to take care of its chief winter meat supply. Supper became magnificent with fresh liver. Every old person not able to keep a pig had gifts of frying and roasting pork. Men and women together smoked the hams; women made head cheese and sausage which they stuffed into old salt bags and left in the cold; little boys ran around with the pig's bladder.

The deer season—October and November—was taken seriously only by young men, and there was some feeling against killing partridges. No family ever kept a whole deer for itself; the children were sent around to the neighbors with great helpings.

Thanksgiving and Christmas were the holidays celebrated most nearly like today. Both were big family parties with splendid meals and comatose phases. Relatives coming from a distance arrived by eleven o'clock in the morning to help the hostess with the dinner; they left by four, because dark was already on the way and they had to get back to feed the stock and do the milking. In between they had sat around the long table and eaten roast pork or chicken with stuffing, potatoes, onions, squash, turnips, hot biscuits, flotillas of jelly and pickles, and at least three kinds of pie, apple, mince, and pumpkin. In town, the ambitious would be eating celery, ordered "from Away" two weeks in advance, and displaying yellow chrysanthemums, brought in with the celery. These luxuries seemed the more interesting because the ground was already deep in snow.

The best rooster on the farm was reserved for Christmas; indeed, when he acted vain he was told of his coming fate. Every house had a Christmas tree: it was only necessary to walk over to the pasture to bring in a fir that touched the ceiling. Children strung ropes of bog cranberries and white ropes of popcorn, mothers hung red apples and lighted candles among the branches. Long black stockings hung in a row beside the fireplace, and the Christmas Eve wore away somehow.

Parents planned to give children a good time at Christmas and to gratify their biggest wishes. They themselves had been Civil War children; they could remember no more than an orange and a home-made doll or top in their stockings. In the morning children, climbing into the parents' bed in the cold darkness, were given the stockings to keep them quiet. After breakfast, the carnival with the tree began.

After cold weather was established, the holidays ended and the pleasures came from breaks in the routine. One recreation was going to town. A woman went once a week, if she felt like it and had the proper clothes. When the sidewalks were icy she wore "creepers" (spikes) on her overshoes. After she had finished shopping, she had no place to go and could only walk slowly to meet her husband in the post office or at the sleigh. Many women never went to town at all. Any man who had nothing pressing to do went twice or three times a week. He could always buy groceries and the newspaper but what he really wanted was to feel the town buildings around him, to mingle with the crowd, and meet other men. The grocery store was his Inn. He might sit all day around the stove, munching crackers and cheese for lunch and coming home full of men's talk. For nine months, from the middle of April, he would be too busy to loaf in a store.

At this time of year, the big spyglass, three feet long, was used almost as a telephone. A family lookout turned the glass on every team driving around a loop in the road over a mile away. When the right horse appeared, the cook would put on the potatoes and gauge the time of serving dinner. Neighbors living far apart had a code, hanging red cloths out of upstairs windows to mean that a sick person was or was not better, a visitor was coming, and so on. Real meddlers sat by the hour turning the spyglass on every team and every pedestrian; it made for conversation.

On stormy days, idleness became part of the slow and limpid flow of time. No one came, no one went farther than the barn, nothing happened, darkness lowered by four o'clock. Then the simplest changes—eating, sleeping, keeping warm—became the pleasures.

Eating at leisure was an evocation of memory and landscape. Just as the lobster tastes of the waves and the sea wind, the New England boiled dinner brought back the summer sun on fields of potatoes, carrots, turnips, and cabbage. Buttering the hot biscuits and spreading mustard on the corned beef, the farmer enjoyed eating his past. The turnips proved his wisdom in breaking new ground; he compared the taste of different kinds of potatoes as a Frenchman compares wines.

Food was heavy, abundant, and well-cooked except for beef with which the cook had little experience. The diet was high in starch and sugar, rich in appetizers and condiments, lacking in salads and fresh fruits, but with cooked fruit at nearly every meal. Meals came punctually, every day at the same times. The tables were set according to rules of design with a white or red-and-white checked tablecloth, silver, glass, heavy white china. Table manners were the mother's constant struggle, with the father's occasional enforcement. Haste was bad form. Children had no incentive to hurry because they had to sit at the table until the adults were through.

A typical winter breakfast would be oatmeal with cream, eggs, hot blueberry muffins, applesauce, and coffee; dinner might be fried ham, mashed turnips, baked potatoes, tomato chow-chow, apple pie and tea; and supper, fish cakes, cole slaw, hot biscuit, ginger cookies, strawberry preserves and tea. Variations included roast pork, salt pork, salt fish, venison, clams, kippers, chicken (on Sundays), baked fish with sage-flavored stuffing, vegetable stews, baked beans, and baked peas. Sweets included mince, apple, pumpkin, squash, custard, berry, and lemon pies; gingerbread; chocolate, banana, and whipped cream cakes; sugar and molasses doughnuts; spiced hermits with raisins and nuts; endless jellies; and sweet and sour relishes. The housewife frequently began to plan the day's menu the moment someone came in from outside saying, "It's 5 below."

Toast was unusual except in illness; hot cornbread and brown bread came weekly. Oranges, pears, bananas, and candy were eaten as evening snacks, not at meals. Butter was very abundant. Milk could have been, but farm children generally hated it; it was only for pigs and hens. Lamb, roast beef, turkey, kidneys, and sweetbreads were not on the menu, and veal was unusual. The meat the farmer brought from town when he could afford it was steak, cut thin, and served well-done with brown gravy.

Diets were unknown; people were supposed to be fat or thin because they were made that way. Those who would now be directed to salt-free or sugarless or fatless diets did not even see the doctor until illness reached an acute form. The only general restriction was that older people sometimes declined the second helping, saying "Fruit cake is a little mite rich for me."

In summer, even men doing hard physical labor got along without meat. Their own pork was gone and the farm did not raise enough chickens for more than Sunday and holiday dinners. The farmer's August dinner might be new green peas and potatoes, shelled lima beans, new corn and beets, new cucumbers floating in vinegar, blueberry pie and tea, with lots of hot bread. Nearly everything came out of his own ground. The wife took it in good part if he ate half a blueberry pie.

Sardines were rejected because a nearby hamlet had a sardine factory and the cannery methods were too careless for good housekeepers. Otherwise, fish was abundant. Kippers were bought in wooden boxes the size of an overnight case. Dried salt cod was always on hand for a meal of fish, salt pork scraps, and boiled potatoes. Ten cents would buy an enormous fish meal from a man who drove to the door all summer with cod, haddock, halibut, and smelts. In the winter he changed to clams. Knowing the size of every family, he opened the back of the pung in the freezing cold and brought to the house whatever he thought reasonable:

eight cents worth for a family of two, twenty-five cents worth for a large family.

A man's lunch when he cut wood back in the forest on freezing days was ham, biscuits, pie, doughnuts, cheese and tea. A child, getting together a school lunch for a rainy day, did not spare the larder. She planned to exchange tidbits with other children. Lunches taken from home to picnics were complicated with potato salad, frosted cakes, and pies trembling under two inches of meringue.

Sleep must have been among the luxuries, because such ample provision was made for it. Winter nights were a white stillness; sleep was as long as nine hours. Windows were not opened. The last wood in the stoves burned to ash about midnight, and people lay quietly from then to morning in heatless houses, behind their storm-windows, storm-doors, and the protecting snowdrifts. The sleeping rooms contained no storage, no reminders of the rest of life; they were white caves made for sleeping. The average bedroom had white walls, white curtains and counterpane, a double bed, a bureau, commode, and several chairs, all in the white silence that favors oblivion.

Parents and guests slept on feather beds, children rustled on straw ticks. Covering was a heavy weight of blankets, and quilts and puffs filled with cotton batting. Small children slept together, but by adolescence they usually had their own rooms and clothes closets. Two boys or two girls sleeping in the unfinished attic had a large cold space under a high roof; they expected to have soapstones put into the bed in the early evening. No one ever read in bed at night. The lamps were blown out, and it was usual to say "I fell asleep as soon as my head touched the pillow." Insomnia was an unknown word.

In a culture which defined so sharply the complementary

functions of the sexes, it must have been a pleasure to know that one was fulfilling one's function. When the blizzard blew, the man, sitting before his open fireplace, could know that he was keeping the family and the stock sheltered and warm. The woman could know that everyone was nourished and clean because of her.

Country life produced such durable human satisfactions that hobbies, now recommended, were rare; some women sewed more than others, some men followed horses. The drift of a hobby was toward making something rather than collecting.

Making presents was regarded as a recreation. Women sewed, knitted, and crocheted for long intervals, saying only that they were making Christmas presents. Men gave presents of fine vegetables, venison, medicinal whiskey; they carved whistles and made carts and hoops for children. Lending was one of the pleasures. Books traveled from hand to hand, magazines and newspapers circulated to three or four houses. Broody hens were lent for a long time to anyone who wanted to raise chickens. Baby calves were sometimes given away, because they were too pretty to take money for.

The great renewals, outside of human relations, had to be, for the average person, work and Nature. Only the exceptional found them in religion. Work gave, over and over, the experience in one's own body of making something from beginning to end.

In a more subtle way, life rose and ebbed with Nature. Everyone had, from the beginning of life, the sense of space. The world around was wonderfully organized in design and the average man or woman had hardly seen anything that was not. From childhood, everyone felt the silence of the forest and knew the sensation of standing in a grove of trees. A man knew that he was not the tallest unit in the landscape. The trees were six times as tall as he and when he cut one down he counted the rings and knew that he was only a pilgrim.

Storms brought a disciplining reflection. Rain affected the crops, snow made hard work, the gold wires of lightning were unanswerable. Anyone out in storms had seen lightning strike trees. Families used to watch rain and snow fall, comparing any great storm with historic storms, remembering from which direction the wind blew years ago. When the storm ended, when the winter ice broke up in the river, when the freshets poured over the falls, the relief from suspense made a holiday for man.

Men were capable weather prophets. A man leaning against a fence rail was not idle, he was studying the wind and the sky in the open. A woman who did not know whether to go to town or not would send a child to some old neighbor to ask if it were going to storm. Children caught in the woods in thunder storms knew that they must not try to go home or to take shelter under the trees. They curled in the open in hollows between grassy banks and let the cold torrents flatten them to the ground.

After a storm, it was a custom to drive over to see the falls in town. It was known that Niagara Falls were 160 feet high and that Machias Falls had not much height, but they were still able to give the feeling of power. The falls had two drops; after the first they churned through a little canyon with clouds of spray, fell again in a white curtain, and roared on in strong yellow suds into the river.

Without going away, everyone experienced, in the weather and the four seasons, wonderful changes. By the time the summer sun became monotonous, fog came to rest the eyes. After the trees were through with yellow and red and russet, they were soon rimed with white. After wearing three pairs of wool socks and rubber boots, the feet could run bare on the grass. Especially as age drew on, the movement from winter to spring to summer to fall and from day to night, night to day, came to be an avowed hold on life.

It seemed as if the most important part of life was spent outdoors, almost as an extension of the landscape. Overhead, masses of cumulous clouds were always traveling the bowl of the sky. Twice a day the sun put magnificent coloring into the east and west. Round about, the hills sloped down to the calm of the river and the marshes. The outdoors was also inside the individual and gave him his definitions of strength, serenity, and beauty.

10

Belief and Code

"I SLEPT AND DREAMED that life was Beauty . . . I woke and found that life was Duty." These words embroidered on the pillow shams were widely approved by the people in the hamlet.

Fashion's last touch to the big white bed in the farmhouse "guest chamber" was the pillow shams. The two white linen squares had pictures and words embroidered in red. The left-hand one showed a girl reclining, asleep under trailing flowers; on the right-hand square she was on her feet, using a broom. A wire contrivance attached to the headboard flipped the shams into the air above the guest's head at night, returned them to position as thought and ornament the next morning.

Something in the countryman sought the contrast of ideas like beauty and duty. Whenever he saw the silken gloss, he began looking for the steel mesh. Flowing through all his pleasures and renewals, of course, he had the left-hand instinct for joy. But he also had a contrary right-hand instinct, subtle and maddening, which warned him not to let joy go too far, not to let the way become too easy, in fact to accept the hard. In some private wind tunnel of his own, his test was to see how much pressure he could resist.

This constant testing of the self perpetuated certain social beliefs and codes, held by everybody. They were not newly made, merely inherited, but their nature was such that the application had to be reiterated in every generation. Attitudes toward the church and school had been institutionalized from early times. Belief and code were equally influential, since they were lived every day.

The beliefs held most firmly were two: first, individualism; second, the continuity of customs approved by long experience.

Individualism meant the person's right to be fully himself, with his corresponding obligations of self-denial and self-control. The customs oftenest under social scrutiny were orderliness, organization, cleanliness, and the use of time and opportunity. These channels were prescribed, but still a person might depart from the standard without hurting anyone but himself; they were not compulsory. No variation was permitted, however, because of the effect on others, in matters of honesty and in sexual mores. These were stiffer than customs; they were the code.

Everyone of every age was an individualist. If the hamlet had ever chosen itself a banner, it could have been that yellow flag with the coiled rattlesnake and the motto, "Don't tread on me."

One aspect of individualism was the passion for saving. Thrift was the other side of the flag of independence. You saved to have more of yourself, otherwise you might have to take directions from other people. This did not negate cooperation, which was old-fashioned and hearty. Folk helped each other greatly in illness, misfortune, old age, and sometimes in poverty; they lent each other the use of land and equipment and argued that all children must have opportunity.

Now that styles come and go so rapidly that half the things one owns often can not be repaired because they are out-dated before they wear out, it is impossible to realize the ardor with which the forefathers once tried to be "saving." If the milkpan sprung a leak, the housewife sat down at once and drew a rag through the hole. If the coffee pot leaked, the farmer, before the next day's breakfast, heated his soldering iron and called for all the old kettles that needed repair.

Debt paved the road to ruin, so the game was to calculate what could be saved by doing without. Very great waste came about from inability to pay for modern farm equipment and fertilizers, but big savings were out of reach, so small deprivations were accepted thankfully, almost like penance, with sayings like "Waste not, want not" and "A stitch in time saves nine."

A caller at a farmhouse could see planned frugality as soon as he entered the outer hall. The broom hung upside down there because resting it on the floor would wear out the straw. The rubber overshoes in a row had large rubber patches. Within the household, clothes, shoes, curtains, rugs, harness, gutters, carriage robes were mended until the substance fell apart. Hoes and shovels had new handles, wagons wore out several pairs of thills, broken stove grates were toggled together with wire, the outside edges of sheets were turned to the middle, napkins were made of old tablecloths, black hats were re-trimmed for twenty years, the unused half of a sheet of letter paper was cut off and saved for another writing.

Of course, at the same time the family was wearing out hand-knitted clothes that would now cost fabulously, the fire-tender was being prodigal with birch logs, the cook was whipping a pint of cream and breaking sixteen eggs into a cake bowl any day she felt like it. Eggs and cream and silver birch were cheap and knitting was only a matter of buying yarn; certainly no one would count labor.

Economy was tied to work and the lazy were "just one step from the Poorhouse." The folk saying about the Poorhouse reveals a fear. The hamlet had never had a Poorhouse, and was not in those years giving any aid to the poor, but still the past cast a shadow. Parents in their schooldays had had to learn by heart a poem called "Over the Hills to the Poorhouse," and they could still repeat the verses. The town had a Poorhouse, and to be in it was regarded as being only second in disgrace to being in the Jail. Any elderly critic could tell the case histories of the inmates and at just what corner in life they took the wrong economic turning.

One of the warnings that the world could end was the foreclosure of a mortgage on a home. It happened only once or twice, but when neighbors read in the newspaper of a foreclosure on an old couple, they grew pale with shock. They knew all about the illness or accident which had kept the mortgage from being paid. Wondering how to show sympathy, they would decide to act as if nothing had happened.

Children were cautioned to save their shoes, clothes, books, and pennies. "And do not wear out your hood swinging it by the strings." They had savings accounts started for them at birth by the grandparents and were told,

"Save the pennies and the dollars will take care of themselves." Birthday and Christmas presents of coins tinkled into their little red iron banks on the sitting-room shelf. The child could shake this bank for excitement, but money once dropped in could not be taken out; not until five dollars had accumulated and it could be taken to the big Bank in town.

Adult savings were laid aside in cash, kept in the name of man and wife in the town Savings Bank. Bills were paid in cash as soon as they were received—unless arrangements to barter had been made. A man might work for sixty years, spending only for family needs and small consumer luxuries, without being able to leave an estate of more than a few hundred dollars. Yet if he had lived a good life and had fine children, he would be counted successful.

The feeling for the individual in one's self was so strong that it protected all kinds of eccentricity in others. Except in an English village no people could have been more tolerant of variations from the norm. The hamlet sheltered its dreamer, its lazy man, its separated couple, its Xantippe, its middle-aged widow with gigolos, its citizens who were just plain queer. The gigolos were thought not respectable, but queer people in general were regarded as interesting: "makes for a change." In a Republican stronghold a voter could turn Democrat with no comment except a thin-lipped, "That is his privilege."

Individualism showed in a good way in treatment of the handicapped. The hamlet had three handicapped people. They were treated, without comment, as much like other people as possible. Two women were cripples, one deformed by tuberculosis and the other by a street accident. Neither was eligible for marriage, but both had paid jobs at the average salary, went to parties and picnics, and were protected without ostentation. The third was an invalid, quiet in behavior but lurching in walk and unable to speak. She could shake hands; so she went to church every Sunday and people shook hands with her without speaking.

The high value put on the individual showed in the attitude toward single women. They were as much at home in the hamlet as they are on college faculties and in metropolitan cities today. They had functions: they lived at home, taking care of aging parents and doing some outside work for pay, like nursing or sewing or teaching. In getting jobs, the single woman had preference over the married.

Men might say gravely that the neighborhood was too small, or that no man whom she had a chance to meet would be good enough for her, but they would not go so far as to say she ought to take a left-over. The idea that young women owed something biologically to the race would have met heavy sarcasm. If a spinster refused a widower with small children, men and women alike said, "Well, why shouldn't she? She is getting to where she can enjoy some life for herself; her father and mother took enough out of her."

Driving the self hard, pinching pennies, and being clean (even if the water had to be carried across two fields) all added up to self-control. Self-control was a discipline, a principle of education, and a panacea. No matter what anyone wanted, doing without was better for him. The baby must not have soothing syrup. The boy having a cut in his head sewn up must not cry. Women should refuse anesthetics at childbirth. The old person dying of cancer would refuse the morphia until the pain broke him.

Maine was still a Prohibition state and many people had never tasted spirits. People had convictions against the use of liquor except in illness and no one ever made wine or cider. The old silver goblets that were the communion cups used to be filled with grape juice.

Smoking was not considered in relation to health but as the indulgence of a useless habit. Young men could not afford to smoke and did not. Not as many as a dozen men smoked, but some of those were addicts: "I smoke only once a day; put her in in the morning and take her out at night." In courting, the girl turned away from the smell of tobacco and the man "swore off" for her. After marriage perhaps he smoked again, but nowhere in the house except the kitchen because the wife said the smell would not come out of the curtains and rugs. Chewing tobacco was regarded as an old man's habit, and repulsive. It was perfectly well known that the mothers of some of the old people had smoked pipes, but that was before people knew better.

The town had two soda fountains, but people in the hamlet did not know what an ice cream soda tasted like. No one could afford to build up "self-indulgence" in ice cream and sodas, and soft drinks were unknown.

Chewing gum could be had any time by walking up to a spruce tree. The pink and honey-colored crystals stood out on the bark; a knife easily dug them off. The neighborhood thought the use of this abundance was a matter for self-control. No one was supposed to chew gum publicly; it was bad manners. Children were warned not to allow gum-chewing to become a habit. "When you begin to need gum, it is time to stop."

Once a day was often enough for coffee. While adults took tea for the other two meals, children were told, "Wait until you're twenty-one." They drank only water or, in winter, cocoa. All stimulants were deplored as taking away from an individual's ability to manage himself.

Eating between meals, except for children and men at hard physical work, was against the theory of abstemiousness. Asked to have another round of pancakes, the guest might reply that he wanted more "but better not, I got to keep the upper hand of myself."

Historically, the colonial settlement had not left matters to self-control, but had multiplied laws and minor prohibitions, chosen law enforcement officers, and compelled them to serve or pay a fine. This phase had passed and was superseded by the very effective controls of custom and public opinion. Neither the hamlet nor the town had a police force. Law was resorted to chiefly for property matters. It was custom that sanctioned everything, saying that all must go "according to law and order."

Order was a virtue, always set as a goal in periods of let-up. Organization was an essential of work. People were rated even within their own families on whether or not they were good organizers.

Organization led into an almost excessive regard for time. In a day, the hours for meals, rising, retiring, and rest or play were fixed. The contacts with school, church, the train, festivities had an allotted time range. The hamlet tended to develop a whole tribal ritual about time. Children who liked to dally had to learn, "Lost! One golden hour set with sixty diamond minutes. No reward is offered, for it is gone forever."

Cleanliness was in a way a component of order and organization. Not everyone could organize—it was a gift—but everyone could clean. Cleanliness brought the flush of ardor, as did work and thrift. The standards of cleanliness for a house, a barn, a hen-house, a carriage, a floor, the inside of a closet or a cupboard were perhaps actually higher than today, when people have less respect for property. Some parts of buildings and equipment were cleaned daily in turn and cleaned with terrible purpose and elbow grease. Women wore themselves "to the bone," as they said, cleaning the whole house twice a year, cleaning hard once a week and again from day to day, but they thought it no more than their duty. Men were less scrupulous, but were always cleaning around barns and outbuildings.

Perhaps the cleaning was an instinctive therapy. Scrubbing and cleaning may have been a refuge from the frustration of life. A person who wanted something desperately could turn to cleaning instead and get so tired that after awhile her only wish was to rest.

The standard of washing clothes was what we know now. Woolens, silks, and heavy coats must have been a problem, since they were not dry-cleaned. Dresses were protected by large aprons, everyday wools were washed, children wore white pinafores over winter wool frocks.

The care of milk, butter, and other food was extraordinarily painstaking for people who knew little about bacteria. The cows' bags were washed, the milker washed his hands and put on a clean apron, the utensils were washed separately, scalded and left in the sun; milk and butter were kept in a special place, screened and secluded. Houses were screened against flies, disinfectant was poured down kitchen drains, wooded sinks were scrubbed white, water was always kept near the boil, bars of yellow soap and boxes of Gold Dust stood on the pantry shelves.

Cleanliness about milk and butter was a matter of the farm's reputation; personal cleanliness was only a matter of family habit. Baths took a long time because of having to carry water and fill and empty a wooden tub. They were a Saturday routine in most houses, but girls and women took sponge baths oftener and barefoot children stumbled out to wash the feet before going to bed. Young people kept combs and brushes and toothbrushes in their bedrooms. The elders sometimes kept them in the kitchen and used them there.

Against the positive habits of industry, economy, prudence, and doing right just to be doing it, instruction on what was bad or wrong was limited and chiefly conveyed by dramatic tales. The hamlet's attitude was rather like the motion picture code: sin must not be shown except in connection with punishment. One woman was known to entertain out-of-town men in the evening. No one would say more than "Good morning" or "Good evening" to this woman. The frightful illness which followed a girl's self-induced abortion was widely talked about. Everyone knew the partner involved, the method, the highest temperature, the glaze of misery; when she got around again, she was ostracized and finally went away.

The hamlet did not have the obvious great sins. Murder was unknown in the area. Crimes of violence against the person, theft, and graft were unknown. The widow and the orphan were not pushed out into the storm. People might covet or hate, but these were private sins. Offenses against the sexual mores and gossip were the local wrong-doings.

The live issue, on which there was thought, instruction, and social judgment, was honesty. At this point, the code began. A man's word was supposed to be binding without anything in writing; for instance, the supplying of all the sand and gravel to be used in a new building was only a question of verbal agreement. Training began early. A child was reproved for disobedience but punished for lying.

People believed in their own local government or else they stopped complaining the minute elections were over.

During the year they would say, "Town Meeting will take care of him." Before Town Meeting, electioneering went on at the grocery, in barns, by the roadside with a foot on the fence rail, and from the wagon seats of two teams going in opposite directions. When the voting was over—voting for assessors, selectmen, tax collector, treasurer, town clerk and superintendent of schools might take a long half-day— the wheels turned as before.

The defection from the truth was in horsetrading. It was not supposed to be honest; it was a game of skill played by two professionals set to do each other down. Women said that horsetrading was wrong but men who liked to dicker about horses paid no attention. A smart trader was said to have swapped horses seven times at Camp Meeting, going home with the horse he started with and $100 to boot. If the buyer were cheated, the procedure was to say nothing, defend the animal to all comers and get rid of him as soon as possible and then do the cheater down on some subsequent trade, much later. Two really confirmed traders would spend two hours arguing, "If you will agree that the horse is worth $100, I will let you have him for $85 cash." . . . "Iffen you will let him go for $85, stands to reason he ain't worth $65. . . ."

Suffering for the sake of doing right was a commonplace and the gospel of endurance was so extreme that nowadays it might seem like masochism. The chief protection against this strictness was the affirmative attitude toward love and marriage. Beginning with romance and extending through all aspects of marital status, to divorce and remarriage after the death of one partner, ideals of love filtered into every corner of daily life and were happy, or at least contented, and romantic in a good sense. Love began with all man's dreams and turned into his stability.

The children of the one-room school once spent their spare time poring over a borrowed Shakespeare, learning the best quotations about love from *Romeo and Juliet*. When one of the older girls came into the yard, they wanted to be able to strike postures and say:

> . . . what light through yonder window breaks?
> It is the east, and Juliet is the sun.

As they went on they could not resist, "O! swear not by the moon, the inconstant moon," and it became an embellishment to leave for home at four o'clock quoting:

> Good night, good night! Parting is such sweet sorrow,
> That I shall say good night till it be morrow.

The Shakespearian research was because the Big Girl in the algebra class was engaged. Love was not much talked about as a theory but when an application came along, parents and even grandparents showed faith in it. The old, who did not believe in religious conversion—they disapproved of evangelists and revivals—and who kissed only children, would still say that love was the clue to life, the young would some day "fall" in love, and everyone would know when his time came.

The position of the sexes could be observed daily. In some marriages the woman was plainly in an inferior position, but again the man could be subservient; sometimes the man and woman appeared equal and complementary. The total effect was of a mysterious union, inevitable.

On the fringe of the woman's talk was the Cinderella wish. They could repeat "Maud Muller" and they hoped for the Judge to pass while she raked the hay. They liked English love stories about Lord X—— bringing his bride in white satin and pearls to the castle. It was women who kept alive the tradition of the hope chest, the importance of the ability to cook and keep house as a preparation for marriage, the Valentine, the engagement ring, the trousseau, and the family wedding; perhaps also the halo around the maiden. Men paid only grudging attention to these trimmings, but a father often said publicly that no boy was going to get his daughter until he had a place to put her and some money in the bank.

Custom inclined toward a late pairing off. Children of both sexes played together until their interests separated in the early teens, but after that girls went around with girls and boys with boys. Hasty attempts to make the girl "ladylike" began. She put on very stiff corsets, her skirts grew long, longer. She was not to "stram around" any more. Certainly no more baseball; she could play croquet, could take drives in the horse and buggy. She was to lie in the hammock in modest positions, she had to fend off the summer sun with a parasol. Probably she was enfeebled by the warnings about effort and bathing during menstruation.

From about the fifteenth or sixteenth year, girls and boys went around together in the evening, in crowds of as many as twenty. All the boys walked all the girls home from church and parties, clutching them by the arm. Old age was coming on—nineteen or twenty—before the matter of a kiss at the doorstep came up. Adolescents heard at home that showing emotion was "too extreme." Walking arm in arm was permissible. Kissing and hugging were not. To put an arm around a cousin as she played the piano for singing was "excessive"; it smacked of lally-gagging and the maudlin; it was "not done."

When a couple began to "go steady," it was a kind of announcement. They spent long evenings sitting up, wearing out the parents who wished the boy would go home. He became capable of giving her a book of Adelaide Anne Proctor's poems in limp leather. They went on Sunday picnics and to far-away dances. The spectators watched hawk-eyed and the chaffing was incessant. The courtship flush of life might last six months; then the young passed into the zone of age and reason.

Marriage as an institution appeared to the young as permanent as the land. Very ordinary folk were admired for the pattern of their marriage, and marriages were talked about, on the whole, in a kindly way. Everyone knew the countless marital glances and gestures—of question, belonging, and reliance.

A man and a girl got married at the girl's house and had a wedding supper, a shower of presents, and a party. After that they drove to their new house, a strip of land with a cow and some poultry. Perhaps the neighbors followed to give them a chivaree; they had to be fed and were hard to get rid of. After the bride had cooked the first breakfast, the groom went away to his work in the fields. On the first Sunday after marriage, if there were church services, they "appeared out" in the bridal finery. From the time of marriage for fifty years, except as the man worked in the woods in winter, they were hardly separated for a meal and never for the night. Changes came: one child, another, another, the addition to the house, the new sheds, a new pasture, different horses and cattle and crops and equipment, sickness, death, the children leaving home. But still this couple rarely appeared in public in their free time except together: socials, church, drives, visits, shopping trips. Their picture in the neighbors' eye was a twin picture, the woman silhouetted against the man.

Various traditions within marriage were customs established by community experience. Family work, spending, and decisions slanted heavily in the man's way, but he had nothing to say about the house except the time of his meals. A woman kept out of barn affairs, but figured in plans about the crops. The man had to build and take care of the hen-house, but he must not even ask about the egg money. He bought the cows, the hay was his, he might even churn if he had time, but he must not interfere with the butter money.

If the functional balance of the sexes was changed by illness, adaptability was admired; otherwise, it was grounds for criticism. Public opinion was so omnivorous that it shored up marriages as an anonymous environment does not. No man was at liberty to be very lazy or feckless; he knew shortcomings would come back and sting him. No woman could look at another man; it would have been all over the hamlet the same day.

Putting everything together, the teen-ager's information about sexuality was considerable. He knew about coition for reproduction from farm animals. It appeared to him as necessity geared to violence, engineered by the owners. He assumed that human coition was for reproduction too, and also difficult and unpleasant; it implied children and everyone knew children could not be properly born outside wedlock. Sexual experience before marriage was reprehensible in men, unpardonable in women. If it were followed by a forced marriage, the couple lost face. Since everyone knew, they might just as well have worn the letter "A" for the rest of their lives; this part of their history could be quoted against them for a generation. The hamlet had seven forced marriages in a decade and three illegimate births. These last were spoken of as the gravest family disgrace.

The mother at once went away to work outside the area and her parents brought up the child.

The first time that most children learned that the marriage tie could be broken was about 1898 when a wife who had divorced her husband "Away somewhere" came home to her parents in the town. This return was regarded as shocking, but still "the husband drank." No adult thought that a wife had to put up with a drunk, so the first divorce was accepted with the creaking of "What is the world coming to?"

The hamlet's one separation was managed so discreetly that all the blame was put on eccentricity. It was said that the wife talked too much and the husband was a silent man, so they became unable to bear each other. Comment affirmed that each of them was showing personality traits of their parents and that they should have known these traits beforehand.

A lot of instruction on the subject of marriage was available to the young, but this was not what is now considered instruction in books. Talks began with economics. Parents said that they did not want their daughters to marry farmers. "We don't want her to be scraping the dish all her life." If girls were to choose such a hard life, marriage had better be delayed until the couple were older. Opinion was against great disparity in age, "never be an old man's darling."

Fostering marriages among the middle-aged was a favorite indoor sport. Bachelors were regarded as hopeless, but spinsters, widows, and widowers had many willing marriage brokers. Good housekeepers must not go begging when a man known as "a good provider" was living alone, trying to cook for himself. Eligible candidates from as far as twenty miles were reviewed, introduced, and blessed.

"My husband," a wife explained, "remembered me from when I was a girl. When I came home to take care of Mother's erysipelas, he had been a widower a long time. He met Father on the street one day and said, 'Is Jane interested in any man Away?' Father said he didn't know, he would have to speak to Mother. So the next time I was going to town Mother said, 'I want you to take a little basket of eggs as a present to Mr. Wood.' So in a little while there I was with her best sweetgrass basket, for him to look over. I never knew about any of it until after we were married."

Remarriage a year after the partner's death was considered reasonable for the young who had a long life before them, but a minority questioned it for those in late middle age. The polite comment was that remarriages in such cases was not respectful to the memory of the dead; unvarnished, it appeared as "No fool like an old fool." Neighbors spending an evening together often used to argue about remarriage. Both men and women could be found who were against all remarriage except for the very young. One winter evening, an old man eating an apple as he sliced it with his jack-knife said, "Love should last beyond the grave." He closed the knife with a snap and continued, "A man must learn to carry his grief."

Regulations concerning social class were not part of the code in the same sense that honesty and sexual mores were, but they still could not be disregarded in marriage without heavy penalties. Class divisions were based on family, money and character. Transplanted from English origins, awareness of class differences had been around long enough to be the very calcium in the bones of the elders.

Although class distinctions were accepted casually, almost mechanically, by parents, they were the weight which most oppressed and confused adolescents. At the very moment when his history book was saying "All men are created equal," he would hear at home that some schoolmate was not a suitable friend, because he came of such poor family stock. He might appear promising when young, but "His grandfather was that sly old Jim Sims, lived on the Dexter place, would lift anybody's eyeteeth." The adolescent always said "I don't care," but he had already observed that social strata and attitudes toward them could not be altered.

Social classes in the hamlet could not be adequately defined by wealth; to apply merely an economic test is too simple. A crude definition on this basis would note that those families near the bottom of the scale had no horse and had to walk everywhere. The middle group owned transportation. The upper group owned transportation and an organ, and were giving their children educational advantages. However, it was possible for a member of the "aristocracy" to own no means of transportation. The rationalization would be that he had chosen better than worldly things, but the person of the lower class did not have enough gumption to buy a horse.

The actual bases of the class differences in the hamlet were not tangible. Everyone owned a house and land; therefore house and land and their location had nothing to do with social status. Neither had race; practically everyone was of the same race and national origin. Religion was not involved; all were Congregationalists. Nor was recent immigration; most of the hamlet's citizens arrived there at birth or by marriage.

Yet there were three social classes. Stratification was almost as if man needed a level to look up to and a level to look down on. Aristocracy is too meaningful a word—the hamlet would have said "upper crust"—but, at the top, seven or eight families were looked up to. Their character or ability or money were so much beyond the norm that their reputations were unrolled as patterns. No one family had to possess all these endowments; one family was valued for one and another for another.

At the bottom, the lowest level, were four or five families, those where illness or bad luck had gotten the upper hand. Their houses, fields, animals, children, and working habits could be seen to be on the down grade. As soon as slipping was established, neighbors began to remember the deficiencies of parents and grandparents and to discount them as "poor stock," lacking in staying power. Very gradually, outsiders who had at first tried to help them drew away; after awhile they were ostracized.

The middle zone of thirty odd families was in a fluid state. People moved up and down in the community's estimation according to character, work, industry, opportunities given the children, and possibly according to marriage. A stranger marrying into the hamlet from the outlying rural districts was not placed until he could be judged on performance.

Character and mentality were under review more continuously than is possible now even for one single family. If people were thought to be well endowed in both respects, money might make no difference. Financial measurement was easily possible, since everyone knew how his neighbors got every dollar. A son who gave up chances to advance to take care of old relatives, or a widow who had lost her breadwinner, could be as highly rated as a person who had money and spent it well. Brains and initiative were so much cherished that if one member of a married couple was exceptionally bright and enterprising, the other would be tolerated in a higher class level. A family could be raised in class standing by having fine children, and lowered if it had stupid ones.

Class lines could be observed in eligibility for marriage and in children's visiting. The aristocratic group might marry into the top of the middle group or go outside the hamlet or stay single. If choice of a partner went below a certain invisible line of attainment, the marriage would be a *mésalliance* and the in-laws would not be on speaking terms. The middle group married within itself if there were enough candidates. The lowest group had to go outside the hamlet, away from the people who would know about its origins.

Over and beyond the hamlet's class system hung the weight of the class difference between hamlet and town. The town "had everything." The country had nothing; it was only living over again the primitive days of the town. The country felt that it was inferior to the town. Country people lived in a cultural Black Belt and bore the minority's sense of being unequal.

A resident of the hamlet sold his product and bought for his needs in the town; he used the town newspaper and its medical and other services. He might even be a more substantial citizen than many townsmen but he would not go the two and a half miles to the town church of his denomination, unless there was some historic meeting for the whole area. The hamlet versus town attitude grew up in the fifty years after their separation. When the church was one, outlying farmers had contributed timber, labor, and the use of their oxen to build it. Now they said it was "too tony." The farm family never went to the Public Library nor to any social organization, except for three couples who went to the Grange. No one in the hamlet exchanged calls with the town, unless there was a family relationship. Courtship and marriage between residents of hamlet and town were all but unknown.

The country feeling of inferiority fed itself on Thomas Gray's "Elegy Written in a Country Churchyard." The mournful cadence of this poem is so rural that it was asked for again and again at recitations by listeners who had no idea why they liked it. Two children could say all the verses.

> Let not ambition mock their useful toil
> Their homely joys and destiny obscure
> Nor grandeur mock with a disdainful smile
> The short and simple annals of the poor.

There were adults who repeated this verse and shook their heads sadly. The musical rhythm somehow confirmed the obscure destiny.

The countryman helped his ego by taking some of his patterns from Boston. Twenty-one of the households were in communication with their forty-six children who had left the area, many of them living around Boston. When the children returned for two weeks in summer, they wore fashionable clothes, better than those to be found in the town shops. They brought guests, rented horses at the livery stable, went in bathing in the river. The grandchildren had a becoming, urban fear of snakes and the woods; they were going to high school and they took violin lessons. It was a liberating force that the summer contact was with urban culture, not town culture. Humor was a weapon. A countryman who had visited Boston could be very funny about the town's rivalries.

For the town had its rivalries for anyone to see and the hamlet's class system was merely an adaptation of the town's. The town had at the top "The 400," a social elite which had dash, money, and style; birth and education probably counted, too, but what cut a swathe was style. A few women in this set were the only leisured individuals.

At the lowest level, the town had "the Puddledockers," defined by residence and religion. They lived on the fringes going toward the country or on Old Maid's Hill or in the oldest housing—once so desirable—near the wharves. Some were Irish and their Catholicism was a fear to Protestants. Numerically this group was small, because a brilliant individual could get out of it; but at the turn of the century, the lowest class could be represented by an Irish Roman Catholic male, no longer young, who had no property.

The hamlet always quoted this classification of social extremes but thought little about the majority in between. A bit more colorless, they were just the "middle-class," merchants, clerks, and salespeople. The small merchant class was disliked, because of its power to drive hard bargains. If the wives of merchants had ambitions about getting into "The 400," dislike grew to enmity.

Historically, there had been a time when Negroes were the lowest class in town. Negro body servants were brought to the town before the Revolution and at least one took part in hand to hand combat in the battle of the *Margaretta*. In 1853, a school for Negroes was built, but in time the colored people died or moved away and the school lapsed. By the 1890's, only one Negro remained in town. Uncle Tom was an old man who jolted along on his truck cart, did ragpicking and odd jobs. The race problem was unknown, and this colored man seemed just like anyone else on the fringe of the lower class. He had scarcity value. Children who had not seen Uncle Tom could not say they had seen a Negro.

For justice, or merely to be contrary, the hamlet had some favorites among the town rich. The old man who was the last lumber capitalist was a fond legend. The miller was another. He lived in a fine house, had money, and sent his children to college, but it made no difference. Everyone called him Jack. Men liked to gossip when they went to buy feed of him. He was a big man and he slung around the great bags of meal and fine-feed and cracked corn with his own hands, and he knew the names of everyone's children.

A summer resident of a neighboring village was actually popular because his way of showing off pleased people who liked horses. He kept a tallyho, with coachman in front, two footmen behind, and the bugle calling every few minutes. His four black horses wore red rosettes on their bridles and the vehicle's pale yellow wheels seemed to skim the ground. Summer dust lay in drifts on the road and the riders wore linen dusters. The women wore veils or were bareheaded in the sun.

This turn-out was loved; no matter if it went by every day, people looked at it. Women who saw the tallyho coming around the bend a mile away would wait behind the parlor lace curtains until it passed; outdoors, however, it would have been gauche to stand up from any garden task or to appear to give more than a glance. This was a Christmas card come to life.

Presumably the hamlet had its rebels against the heavy framework of custom. The two suicides and the two insane must be remembered, even if they chose to become mute. The hermit did not write his *Walden*, but he lived it until he died. There were also the invalid who sat in her room all day, the man who read all night, the man who read Latin, the fellow who did rum-running to Canada, and the mighty walkers. All of them could have been doing more authorized things. Their variations, usually dismissed as sickness or laziness, express some dispute with the norm.

But all of these rebellions were of middle age. The young, so far as gossip knew, did not rebel. The loud verbal protests of the young which plague parents were no problem. A plausible reason could be that the young always expected that within a few years they would migrate and be on their own.

11

Arts

THE QUINTESSENCE of a culture of the past, books say, will
live in the arts of its people. This could be partially true of
the hamlet, but only by greatly modifying the customary
notions about the seven arts.

If their houses were to be excavated many years hence,
perhaps; if recordings of their Town Meetings or of their
first soprano singing a Moody and Sankey hymn could
be discovered, perhaps; if one of their home-made wooden
sleds were set in the snow between the evergreens again,
perhaps.

"Perhaps," because they did not originate their architecture or music or crafts or political devices; they made
good adaptations. The hamlet was only a fragment of a
civilization; its handful of families reproduced models of
an earlier period, but were not part of any creative main-
stream within their own culture. The arts of the world's
inheritance reached the hamlet only as tenth degree echoes

185

long after the original voice was heard. Although the role of the countryman was limited to repetition and appreciation of these echoes, a more searching look will show that, in his own way, the countryman was creative.

The success of their lives in a cold country on stony ground is very English; so is their reserve toward the arts. Spirituals, dancing, and island arts produced in isolation come from other climates, conditions, and temperaments. These people were too set on subsistence goals, too reined in emotionally, to create anything out of their deepest selves. The hamlet was a body of life and character. Assuredly it had the substance from which the arts come. But it lacked within itself example, tradition, pattern, technique, supporting public; so its deepest self remained buried.

Its citizens were striving for conduct, not art. They were creating themselves, by rules, by conflict, by appreciation, by recognition. Many of these unknown lived well, died well—silent, consistent, and organized to the end. Some of them talked well. In gossip, in humor verging on satire, and in certain attitudes toward personality, they were creative. This stage of artistic development was not peculiar to the hamlet. It appeared again and again in the building of new towns in the West.

Yet it can be seen that there was some readiness for art. Everyone could do something in the practical arts, men in farm crafts, women in household arts. Everyone was supposed to excel in one or two of the tasks of his routine. Those who did not were called "gormless," which meant lacking in sense of form or in an ability to achieve it. The standard of the ordinary task included the organization, skill, finish, and style that mark the artist.

The graphic arts were the least effective of all the arts;

it can be said that they hardly touched life at all. Painting, except on china or velvet, was unknown. "Pictures" in color reproductions were fairly common. One home had a vaporous reproduction of Murillo's *The Immaculate Conception*, five by three and a half feet, hanging alien and alone on the woodshed wall. Children asking why the picture was so strange were told, "Because it comes from a Catholic country."

The oldest households had illustrated versions of the Lord's Prayer, the Garden of Eden, or the Tree of Life and still-lifes of flowers and fruit, all framed in black. The figures in these pictures had an enchanting rigidity and the backgrounds were rich with design, but the daughters of the house had looked at them so long that they hated them. When they set up their own housekeeping, they became Romantics and hung very large reproductions of *Rock of Ages*, *The Maiden*, or Landseer's *Stag at Bay*, pictures with clouds and much empty space. When the old home broke up and they disposed of "Mother's things," they put her pictures "up attic."

Fragmentary as experience with the graphic arts was, there was something intense in the people's response to photographs. No one had a camera, but every home had many family pictures. They were considered real. After a death, those who remained felt a magic in the likeness. "I keep the boys' pictures where I can see them every time I go down cellar. They live in me while I am looking and thinking about them."

Sculpture would not have been recognized by that name. The figure of the Civil War soldier leaning on his musket was real. Standing on the pedestal in front of the Public Library, he was absorbed into the vison much as the oldest willow was. No one connected him with art and certainly not with the manufacture of statues in Germany. People read into his sad pose their own reflections about war.

Dancing had been influential as a schooling in grace and manners up to the time of the Civil War. Family attendance at dances continued into late middle age. Daughters of the 1870's could tell of their first minuet with their fathers at a New Year's Eve ball. After the change to the waltz and other less formal dances, fewer adults danced. By the 1890's couples did not go to dances after marriage, and dancing as an art was spoken of lightly. It was no more than a way for young people to meet partners and have a good time.

Drama fed the lives of country folk, but not from the stage; it was from real life. When a man who had been haying all day heard, as he left the field, of an accident, an elopement, or a financial coup, the event was so near his life that he did not need other theatricals. He felt the shocker by himself and prolonged his reactions by telling them and hearing others tell of theirs. Love stories and marriages were so nearly an open book that each was everybody's drama. Fear, anger, revenge, grief, and desperation paraded before the eyes or within the hearing often enough to satisfy the need for emotional data in the raw. Talk and reflection folded them into experience.

Children who had never seen a theater invented one with situations, dialogue, and stage properties. First, running with whips of alders or willow herb branches, they were race horses. Then their carts were racing sulkies, the boys horses, the girls drivers. In time they went on through Noah's Ark, cowboys, going West in the covered wagon, De Soto at the Mississippi, being lost on the Sahara, and the Prodigal Son. Under the influence of reading they produced *The Blue Flower* and finally *East Lynne*.

East Lynne was forbidden by parents and it dealt with a forbidden situation, so it was twice sweet. The Lady Isabel, the divorced first wife, changed by age, illness, accident, and dark glasses, returned to her husband's house as governess to her own children, after the second wife and the second set of children were in possession. First came the debutante scene, with the Lady Isabel in white satin, a string of pearls, and evening cape, pausing before Lord Vane: "Good night, Papa." Then came the wedding, the first son named for his grandfather, the little house. In the next act, no one ever wanted to play the villain who carried Lady Isabel away at night, but there was much pleasure in the pandemonium that followed. The deserted husband even changed the daughter's first name; "Never call her Miss Isabel again, her name is Lucy."

The deathbed scene was sometimes played two or three times, because everyone liked it so much. When Lady Isabel lay dying with her dark curls spread out on the pillow, the former husband recognized her. Listening to the reasons for her return in disguise, he was stirred with feeling: "He knew what it was—a longing to kiss her." But *East Lynne* was written in 1860; even to the dying, the hero could give no kiss. The players, all of them under twelve years old, always thought this was hard, but they kept to the book. Their precocious acquaintance with this novel came about from its wide popularity in paper editions. It could be found in homes which had no children's books more advanced than *Mother Goose*.

The one major art apparent on every hand was architecture. The eighteenth century houses had comfortable certainty. Some of them were wonderful examples of the builder's art: the way the mass rose from the ground, the roof sloped, and the proportions blended with the boulders rising from the fields. They were only adaptations of historical models, perhaps built by neighbors under the direction of a carpenter; probably the technique of building in this style had been lost by this time. No construction at all was done in the hamlet during this decade.

New buildings in the town were judged by whether they were large, whether they had ornaments. Couples who had inherited their grandfather's house were already craving something more elaborate. New furnishings of debased line, material, and workmanship were bought with no thought that they would clash with the historic setting.

The flower gardens in the front yard were pleasant repetitions of each other, all very much alike and like those of the past; they were more scientific than artistic. The household crafts, executed with much skill, were also reproductions of the historic. Hooked and braided rugs in home-dyed wool and quilts in many patterns had heirloom quality.

Collections, which are sometimes an index of taste, were seldom begun in the hamlet. The only collections were of autographs, books, pictures, items for scrapbooks, and jewelry. Autographs were a fad, the only one shared by both grown-ups and children. Albums of them in yellow plush covers lay around on parlor tables, and everyone read them through and wrote his name. Adults wrote noble sentiment—"Not failure but low aim is crime." Schoolmates wrote doggerel:

> When you get old
> And cannot see,
> Put on your specs
> And think of me.
>> Sincerely your friend,
> > Jas. McFee Townsend

Books were bought, by book lovers who were mostly women, one at a time after long planning. The same women, or others like them, cut verses out of newspapers and magazines and pasted them into scrapbooks. Other scrapbooks held historical news items and pictures of flowers, many from seed catalogues. These scrapbooks were important. In the last illness a grandmother left hers to the most literary grandchild, so it still may be that they contained the beginning of all collections.

To have jewelry was every woman's ambition, and every man's too because he wanted to give it. As art, it was created elsewhere; in the hamlet its possession was chiefly an economic measurement. Probably only about half the women had more than a single piece of jewelry. People had to be "comfortably fixed" to own watches; perhaps one in three adults owned one. They were Elgin gold watches, the woman's worn on a long gold chain tucked into her belt, the man's on a gold chain strung across his vest.

Older people had pins as jewelry; the women had cameo brooches or red coral branches in gold loops, the men gold dollars mounted as stick pins. Rings were by no means common, except for women's wedding rings. Young fiancées had engagement rings, a garnet in a high claw setting, or a circle of turquoise around a pearl. A diamond was out of reach. Opals used to be longed for, because it would be daring to wear an unlucky stone, but after a girl who wore an opal was burned to death they were feared. Once in a while a daughter in her teens had a gold bracelet and a gold locket or a little gold ring with a raised design; she wore the locket on a black velvet ribbon or on the gold chain given her in babyhood.

Because jewelry was not to be taken for granted, children used to look forward to owning some. School children used to make lists of all the jewelry they could remember in the hamlet, and the worst thing parents could do at Christmas was to give the useful pair of overshoes and withhold the gold ring.

Music was the popular art. Except for religion and human relations, music was the only easy emotional outlet. The content was limited but the response of people lifted out of themselves lasted at least into middle life. Music had terrific lasting power then, and not only the classics but even poor music continued indefinitely to be popular.

About every third family had a reed organ. A local teacher gave lessons and girls learned to play hymns, marches, waltzes, "The Flower Song," McDowell's "To a Wild Rose" and Nevin's "Narcissus." There were no other musical instruments, except for the mouth organs which boys had spells of playing.

Folksongs dating from as far back as 1800 were still sung: "Hole in the Ground," "Sourwood Mountain," "Billy Boy," "Shenandoah," "Go Tell Aunt Rhody." There was a hunger for Irish and English songs like "Wearing of the Green," and "Believe Me if all Those Endearing Young Charms." The mournful was almost a cult; every year "The Last Rose of Summer" dragged to a slower and slower tempo.

Women knew the popular songs of an earlier day, like "The Mistletoe Bough," "We Parted by the Riverside," and "Give my Love to all at Home." Collections of Stephen Foster, English ballads, and standbys like "Juanita," "Clementine," "Little Brown Jug," and "There is a Tavern in the Town," came with the organs and sifted around to everyone. A Spanish-American war song "Just before the Battle, Mother" went on faithfully for five years.

The popular song which introduced the new era must

have been "There'll be a Hot Time in the Old Town Tonight." People as hoarse as crows and long past singing age
took an active part in the controversy about it; they did
not wish to admit that there could be a Hot Time. Parents
forbade the song; it was vulgar. Young men were the only
group unquenched; on the road home after dark, they sang
lustily, snapping out "My Baby" at the end.

The favorite hymns were a mixture of the sublime and
the sentimental, chiefly from Moody and Sankey's *Gospel
Hymns*: "Jesus, Lover of my Soul," "Nearer my God to
Thee," "At the Cross," "Just as I Am," "There is a
Fountain Filled with Blood." The impassioned hymns must
have had many kinds of meaning; the young were learning
about human love from them at the time the old were learning resignation. Youth seemed to prefer hearty singing to
anything else, and some of their favorites were hymns poor
in thought, poetry, and music.

Everyone's life was touched by literature in some form,
although there was a scarcity of printed books. Oral literature was the only art form popularly created in the hamlet.
Dreams, gossip, superstitions, proverbs, obituaries; all the
tales that are told long before they are written down; in
these forms literature reached everybody. There was a
legend about a man crossed in love, which in some other
setting might have become a ballad. Barney Lowe was a
bachelor with a terrible mother. When he was young she
would not let him have Celia, when he was older she contrived to break off his plans to marry Ruth, when he was
middle-aged she made fun of his attraction to the young
Jessie. This story was varied and exaggerated, built to a
climax; but it stopped short of being made into a song.

The number of books owned was perhaps five in an
average family, fifty to a hundred among bookish people.

The Sunday School had a little library of the Esther Reid series and similar pious books for teen-aged girls, but otherwise the only way to have books was to own them. They had to be ordered at the town bookstore "from Away," and it took a long time for them to come.

Children began well enough with *Mother Goose*, "The Frog Who Would a-Wooing Go," and "Red Riding Hood." For birthdays and Christmas, they acquired the *Chatterbox*, *Little Women*, and the Henty stories. Around the house, they could find the Bible, *Pilgrim's Progress*, Longfellow's *Poems*, and a Dickens' novel.

The leanness of reading matter was partly deliberate. Fairy tales were dangerous for children, might teach them to lie. Novels were a waste of time, they rotted the mind. Among the books lent from house to house were Dickens' *A Child's History of England*, Mrs. Humphrey Ward's *Robert Elsmere*, Scott's *Waverly*, *Bear Hunters*, Longfellow's *Poems*, and Hawthorne's *The House of the Seven Gables*. These books were read all to pieces, so that sometimes the owner had to tell the borrower what was on the missing pages.

This New England strain never had any trouble understanding Hawthorne. The town had just such a little sweet shop with a bell above the door and the owner living in the back. Judge Pyncheon appeared a natural figure and people could quote the places about Maule's blood to drink. Hawthorne may have been easier to understand because the hamlet itself was inclined toward mysterious interpretations. The ticking of a certain beetle in the wall meant death. Heard in the stillness of a winter night, it was called the death-watch beetle. "It ticked the winter Grandfather died."

The dreams oftenest told were about the dead. Dreamers

used to talk about the departed as being on earth in spirit, quite in the line of Hawthorne and Poe. Dreams were told as part of the breakfast conversation—every morning except Sunday:

> Saturday night dreamt,
> Sunday morning told,
> Sure to come to pass
> Before the week's old.

It was always felt that dreams meant something but, since arguments got nowhere, dwelling on dreams was only a way to arouse antagonism. One woman had a *Dream Book*; the very possession of it was called proof of a weak mind.

Superstitions had a vogue, without anyone's knowing which ones were believed and which said by rote. Seeds were wrapped in a complicated set of beliefs; they had to be planted in accordance with the moon. The way to cure an asthmatic child was to cut a lock of hair from the crown of his head and put it into a timber of his house at his height. When the child grew above that height, the asthma would be gone. Handling frogs and toads brought warts; but rubbing them with stolen meat and burying it in the ground would take the warts away as the meat decayed. Breaking a looking-glass meant seven years of ill fortune; and if a baby saw his face in a looking-glass before he was a year old, he would never live to have the first birthday. The rooster crowing three times at the doorstep meant an approaching guest; accidents came in threes; starting a trip on Friday was unlucky. Walking under a ladder brought bad luck. An early sign of protest in an adolescent might be deliberately walking under a ladder.

Youth shrugged about these sayings, but liked amusing fragments: "February Ground Hog Day, Half your meat and half your hay," and "Red sky at night, sailor's delight; red sky at dawning, sailor take warning." They disliked "Green Christmas, fat graveyard," and could hardly endure "What is to be, will be" and "Whatever is, is right." The reason young people sometimes accepted old saws could have been that the elders, in telling them, appeared so much more dramatic and convincing than usual. Their expression and gestures became freer, their speech went into the vernacular. "He didn't just fall down, he went stern over crockett."

No one in the neighborhood was known as a humorist. Slapping the knee and doubling up with laughter were foreign manners, yet people were born to the dry and pithy response, the kind of twist called Yankee humor: "I've plenty of money for old age if I die when I'd ought to." Humor was a form of power as harsh as the slap in the face the Zen Buddhist teacher gives to those who ask silly questions. It was usually against something and had a very good chance of getting the upper hand. Because everyone knew how to assert himself by being a little funny, the masters of this craft were able to wield satire. The hamlet so enjoyed racy talkers, it is a pity no one knew about Dr. Samuel Johnson.

Anything in the air that did not travel by word of mouth got around by the newspaper. The six-page weekly was full of facts: births, deaths, marriages, parties, meetings, sales, crops, school, church and lodge news, illness, who had supper or spent the day with whom. The beginning of creation came when these factual items were interpreted and drawn out at great length by the readers.

The most exciting news from the outer world in this decade was the Spanish-American War, as told in the

Boston newspapers, with the saying "Remember the Maine."

Near home, the sensational news was the murder, in 1896, of the Captain, the Captain's wife, and one of the mates of the barkentine *Herbert Fuller*. The same conditions could have fitted the small vessels which came into the town's harbor; the barkentine's home port was nearby; and someone had known the Captain. During the trial, men argued the case for half days at a time, especially about whether the Harvard student passenger could be suspected and whether the wheel could have been lashed long enough for the helmsman to kill three people. Gossip translated the newspaper facts a little, explored and embroidered them in the manner of literary record. After a little, the average person could not remember where he got his information. To hear interpretive gossip from those with the knack was a pleasure comparable to listening to radio big names today.

The lurid local event was a fight between a father and several grown children. Screams pierced the dark night, neighbors were drawn in. Different versions got around of who began it, who said what, who struck whom, the injuries, the roles played by women and mediators. A motherly woman trying to soften the father while things were cooling off said, "I have been married to Enoch for thirty years and he has never given me a cross word." The father was walking up and down holding a wet towel to the place where he had lost a tooth, but he stopped walking: "In course not. He don't dare to." This incident was described, analyzed, revised, and repeated for years, probably for the same reasons that people still go to see *King Lear*.

The best story tellers were women. The most fluent talker in the hamlet was Aunt Hannah. She was one of the aged, ground between the millstones for so long that even her gossip had become an oral work of art.

Aunt Hannah came to the community as a bride in the 1850's, the bright day. The Civil War struck her down and left her bare. She was around until she was eighty-two, but she really died at about thirty-eight. After the passing of her real life, since the body was still here she recovered bits of herself slowly, and her second life consisted of making tales. She looked for the dark side, the fearful worst, the impending Fate. As one shelterless, she took away all shelter from others. Yet this old woman was the only person I ever knew who, over a period of forty years, was formed by grief and loneliness.

When she was young, she was Hannah, married to Nathan. Theirs was the house on the hill, half a mile from any other, the last house in the hamlet. Beyond their land the woods began. Loons lived on the lake nearby and deer and foxes made winter trails across the pastures.

Nathan went to the Civil War, came home wounded after Bull Run, and died of tuberculosis within a year. Nathan Junior caught tuberculosis from his father and died at seventeen. The younger boy, Tommie, got "galloping consumption" that took him off at fourteen.

The three graves appeared one by one in a little burying ground in the fields, four hundred feet below the house on the hill. Every time she looked out of the living-room windows, the wife and mother could see her family in their new place. She used to stand looking at them when she got up in the morning and again the last thing before she went to bed. By moonlight, the marble tombstones showed white against the blackness of a pine grove. Every Memorial Day she laid long apple-blossom boughs over the two Nathans and fashioned small bouquets for Tom.

For the forty-four years of her widowhood she lived alone, in her house between an orchard and open fields, backed by rocky pastures wooded with evergreens. The thin grass in the fields was running out in daisies, cinquefoil, and tawny hawkweed. Patches of wild strawberries, blueberries, huckleberries, and raspberries grew larger and larger. Shrubs and bracken, wild pear, wild cherry, cerise lambkill, and mullein were choking out other growth. Beside the stone doorstep of her house, a yellow rose twisted and climbed.

After the trek across the pasture and the turn around the yellow rosebush, the visitor came into a large entry, pine-paneled, dark with age, empty. The next door opened into the living-room. This room was a white cavern—white floors, walls, counterpane, pillow shams—into which, when she was between seventy-five and eighty, she gradually withdrew. She ate, lived, and slept there, in winter close by the stove and the woodbox. When she went to the pantry for food or to the woodshed for kindling, her footsteps echoed through the unfurnished bedroom and kitchen. The living-room was large and sunny, shining clean and always in order. The maple fourposter, the gate-legged table, and the high slat-backed rocking chairs were consistent; no cushions, no tidies, no ornaments. She had no clock and told the time by the sun or the light.

Probably she lived on a widow's Civil War pension, but the ten dollars or so she spent a month was partly from her own earnings. Her land had no care beyond some thinning out of the woods; it was rapidly returning to pasture. Her house was grey and paintless. Taxes on it were $3.64 in 1900. She never had any new clothes; she always wore the same grey print or black cashmere with white at throat and wrists. Her two black shawls, the thick wool and the thin cashmere, were put on and off according to the season. She went away from home only as far as she could walk. her needs seemed to be only for food, fuel, taxes, and light.

Fuel she got by bargaining with someone to cut and saw wood on her land—on shares. For light, she used only a cupful of kerosene a week. For food, she knitted men's grey socks and children's long black stockings and bartered them for milk, butter, and eggs. She dyed old clothes in gay colors and, from the cloth, braided rugs and pieced patchwork quilts, which sold unquilted for $2.50. She planted and tended potatoes, beans, carrots, beets, corn, squash, and pumpkins—any vegetable at all that, scratched into the ground, would grow without much care. One of her dinner standbys was a vegetable stew called a hudaley and another was parsnip stew. Her chief food, besides bread, eggs, tea, baked beans, and jam, must have been the meat, fish, clams, and sweets sent weekly by the whole neighborhood. Every child in the district knew the path under the balm-of-Gilead trees and the ache in the arms from carrying a piece of pork, a pumpkin pie, and a small loaf of cake. Women who had carried food to Aunt Hannah when they were young were now sending their children.

Sometime after her seventy-fifth year, the old lady stopped going to church. Sunday became the day she did not sew or go berrying. She began to stay alone for Christmas and Thanksgiving then, and her winters were spent "hibernating," as she said, "with the woodchucks." Snowdrifts piled over the fences and rose three feet high in front of her door and on her path to the road. She could not do anything about it; she had to stay in the house until the spring melting.

In summer, she came to life with the yellow rose. From

June to September she ranged over her land, dress pinned
up and black sunbonnet squashed on her head, sniffing out
every last corner, gardening, picking berries, and floating
on her sense of property.

After the autumn leaves turned, callers came to be her
amusement. A mother had to prepare a child for Aunt
Hannah, just as the lawyer explains courtroom tactics to
the witness: "When she asks how much we paid for the
new horse, tell her you don't know. Tell her the pig was
killed yesterday morning at half past seven, and the Parker
House rolls just came out of the oven this morning." The
old lady would surely ask about the horse and if Father had
paid boot. But first she would open the packages—and woe
to any messenger who brought a gift more than a day old.
The recipient was still capable of saying, "Take it straight
back to your Mother. I don't want to have a touse with
stale food."

She was Irish and German in racial origins and she
started life with a powerful memory, a gift for drama, and
a stiff arrogance. These qualities led her to develop a system. She began to talk about the first house in the hamlet,
skewered it with a thrust, passed to the next and damaged it
as much as possible, and so traveled up the road, house by
house, to the community's end.

"Did you folks hear that Jot Gatch has been arrested for
selling liquor? Mealy-mouth that he is, I wonder how he
liked the bracelets on him . . . Ayeh . . . Maine a Prohibition state and him disgracing us all running rum over the
border . . . It all goes back to his mother marrying into
that trifling Gatch tribe . . . Ugly as a mud fence she was,
likely it was her only chance . . . Still Asa Gatch was a
poor stick; didn't have sprawl enough to buy a horse and

wagon all the days of his life, had to walk to town and calculate how to sponge a ride back. . . .

"Don't it take the cake that Elmer Mack and Sarah Lee have got married? All those buggy rides to dances clear to the next Plantation . . . likely it was time . . . High time. . . Shingles falling off his mother's mangy old house, he don't strike a lick, but he has to bring home a wife. He's near and he's lazy; that's how he started and that's how he'll end . . . Well, Sarah was a dunce at school, she got it from both sides . . . We'll see now how smart she is at bending over the washtub. . . .

"Your Mother used to go to school with Sabriny, have you heard what they say is the matter with her? She wouldn't be took to that place without she was losing her mind, I know that as ever I had to eat . . . She never was too strong in the head, always yeeing and yawing, and it's about time now she was having trouble, she's forty-five. Her father used to get as crazy as a coot every spring, walk way to the lumber camps he would and rant to the lumber jacks. . . .

"I never in my born days heard of a worse how-do-you-do than Jim White's boy molesting Minnie right in her father's house . . . Seems as if she must be kind of feather-headed, not minding her p's and q's . . . He ought to be lambasted neck and crop, but maybe if he was, he would go clear off the handle . . . That boy began to go queer the time he ran away when he was in school, working his board at the livery stable. I notice the men that hunted the woods for him them two days said that next time he could lay out; run backwards he did to put 'em off the track . . . It was just women that tried to smooth it over. Whether he studied too hard or not, the livery folks got rid of him . . . I wouldn't trust him any further than I can see through a sifter."

If Aunt Hannah could not damn the contemporary by its own evidence, she could find something damning from ten years ago; if a decade failed, she could go back fifty years. Her cutting edge was sharpened by living in a day when there was no middle course between right and wrong. She believed in sin.

Probably she also believed in conversion. When she made pastry she used to croon snatches of old hymns, "Step into the current and thou shalt be whole," and with a cracked voice she sang as if she saw everything in pictures:

> The dying thief rejoiced to see
> That fountain in his day,
> And there may I though vile as he
> Wash all my sins away.

This old face and figure, whether she was humming tunes or picking cranberry beans, could reveal that old age has its distinctive beauty. She was very tall. She had a confident posture and a look of assurance and dignity. Her expression showed both the creator's happiness and the critic's acid. Her thick white hair, parted in the middle and coiled low, was naturally curly. The dark eyes glittered with fierce life; she did not even own a pair of spectacles. The long and thin face, patterned with fine wrinkles, had deep hollows in the cheeks. The gaunt body, refined down to the bony structure alone, was an elaboration of the face. The hands, long and thin too, with the liver spots and the thin wedding ring like a piece of gold thread, used to clutch a little at the gifts of meat and the bottles of cream for whipping. But Rembrandt used to make portraits of such old women and she was as worth painting as any.

She must have had excellent health. She had no illnesses that anyone knew about, made no complaints, had no doctor. She disapproved of dosing with patent medicines. Women who took Lydia E. Pinkham's medicine or Peruna could hear from her that you could not find ambition in a bottle. In a climate and period when rheumatism was king, she did not have rheumatism. When she waked on winter mornings her wood fire had been out for more than half the night; she had to build it again, but she did not have the winter colds and la grippe. She was accident-free. She used to climb around on ladders to shut upper windows. Every stick of wood she burned had to be carried from the cold woodshed in all weather. She did it successfully all her life.

Perhaps her health was good because she held on so to the savor of food. Eating alone had not dulled her appetite. Her thin old spoons were coin silver of the 1840's, her mended damask was freshly creased, her blue and amber pressed glass was shining. Her hot mince pies, jellied chicken, and spiced crab apples had piquancy. She liked to make a fine meal for a child and did it exactly as she would have for an adult.

If this old woman feared poverty or illness or man she never gave a sign. In the evening she lighted only one small kerosene lamp and very early her hilltop house darkened into the night's darkness. Her doors were never locked, night or day. Every pail of water she used had to be pulled up from a deep open well in the cellar and she used to stand on the edge of this black pit and talk about something else as she turned the windlass.

She never once said that she was getting near the end. Waving good-by from her doorway she gave the feeling that she was as sure as the pines, but she went suddenly. Her life lasted from 1824 to 1906—forty-five years after her mortal wound at Bull Run. After her death her house caught fire and burned to the ground.

Her legacy was to her neighbors. She obliged them to work out an understanding of her tragedy and a method of enduring her vengeance. They knew that Aunt Hannah's tongue was the fire at which she warmed herself. She was regarded as outside of life and its rules; rather in the same class as the Union soldier's statue. But she had in her the stuff that makes art. Probably she could write only a little. She came into the area as a child, walking and riding a pack horse on the trails before roads were cut through; she could remember how the spruce and hemlock boughs pricked the rider as the horse plodded through the evergreens. The school of her day must have been very limited. Therefore her Spoon River Anthology of the hamlet was only spoken, so it too is long gone.

A proper statue of Aunt Hannah would refuse the calm of granite—much of it as she owned—and the elegance of the marble she bought for her three gravestones. She would return to the world most suitably in some glittering black medium, very hard: basalt or obsidian. She needs sharp straight lines. The anguished gashes that the primitives cut for facial expression would become her well.

The old men of the hamlet provided no such Voltaire. They were mild, optimistic, wise, venerated. A few of them functioned as living works of art, because each one stood for something. Each was the best embodiment of courage or mind or goodness that his neighbors knew.

While they lived, the hamlet had, within its body, its "Marseillaise," its "Thinker," and its Hercules.

When migrants from the hamlet dreamed of home, they longed equally for the beautiful view and the tall people.

12

Migration

"FROM EARLIEST CHILDHOOD the boy was accustomed to feel that for him, life was double. . . . Town was winter confinement, school, rule, discipline; straight gloomy streets piled with six feet of snow in the middle. . . . Town was restraint, law, unity. Country only seven miles away was liberty, diversity, outlawry, the endless delight of mere sense impresssions. . . . Winter and summer then were two hostile lives and bred two separate natures. Winter was always the effort to live; summer was tropical license."

The Education of Henry Adams is describing here the effect of two homes—Boston in winter, Quincy in summer —upon a nineteenth century boyhood. Many Americans of that period share with Adams the memory of this double life: the city during the school year, and the home at sea-shore or farm during the summer.

As a place, the hamlet too felt that life was double. In addition to its own stationary life between the hills, there was a second life by migration. The economic resources of the locality were not only the woods and the land; the third way of making a living was by migration. At twenty-one, the young flew away like birds.

Migration began as stern necessity, but time had eased conditions. By the 1890's, migration was sometimes two-way, the young going away to make new homes in the city but returning in summer, the parents going up to the city in the winter. Whether the parents moved or not, both age groups lived in two places psychologically. It was not quite like the psychological division of the twentieth century caused by living in the suburbs and working in the city, but it had points of similarity.

The duality of life was as important to the hamlet's feeling about itself as the city-country experience was to individuals. In popular feeling, home held the same position as Henry Adams' winter while "Away" was his summer. He said that winter was the effort to live, summer was tropical license. We said that life at home was "the hard pan"; life "Away" was opportunity, money, city lights.

From about the middle of the nineteenth century, our forebears' imagination began to be drawn to the West beyond the Mississippi River. Later, from the close of the Civil War to the 1890's, realism determined that the practical goal was Boston.

Farming people were interwoven with the life of the town; many went there every week, rolled town affairs upon the tongue; and yet beyond a point all felt chilly barriers. The fir trees might have come down off the hills and frozen to their full height between town and country. The countryman obstinately felt that the townsman did not regard him as an equal.

No such cleavage applied to Boston. The Boston metropolitan area was faith and promise. When the children were twenty-one they would set out for the Hub. After they were settled they would found their own homes and families there and come home to the hamlet every August, with children, bicycles, and trunks, to a carnival of drives, picnics, and parties. When the parents were "well-along," they might go up to spend winters in the warm city house with its bathroom and electric lights. In between the exchange of visits would be the succession of letters, newspapers, snapshots, boxes of cookies, presents, and money orders. Both children and parents assimilated the two bases of life and, when they exchanged the annual visits, experienced great luxury of fulfillment.

Our next door neighbors, who had seven children in Waltham, Massachusetts, lived alone in a large house, but really only for six months of the year. In late November they boarded up the windows and left, to spend Thanksgiving with one child, Christmas with another, and they kept on making the rounds until April, returning to the hamlet in time for Town Meeting. The next three months were spent putting in the garden and preparing for the shoals of children and grandchildren who would come to visit in July and August.

During the ten years 1894–1904, twenty-one (of the fifty-one) households had forty-six children settled elsewhere. Twenty-two of them were in Boston and its vicinity; one family had six children scattered between Boston and Concord. Seventeen were in the larger cities of Maine, three in Minnesota, and two each in California and Nova Scotia. The thirty homes which had no migrants were childless, or they had enough means for the young to work at home and marry locally, or they had only small children whose migration would come later.

Plans for migration began early. Barefoot children playing in the brook made up games about the time when they would be old enough to go away alone on the train. They all knew that the land was not fertile enough to be divided any more, that work in the woods was only for winter, and that the mores were against doing odd jobs or housework in the town.

The King's original land grants to the settlers had been exhausted by the fourth generation, about 1870. In that year, the hamlet, which had numbered 294 in 1850 just after it was separated from the town, climbed to its population peak of 350 people; by 1900, it had fallen to 227; by 1940 it reached the lowest figure, 173. In 1950, the population had risen to 221, only six less than it had at the turn of the century.

The grandparents, the "Man and Woman" of the first chapter, are representative of the hamlet's experience with migration. They stayed where they were, feeding on the environment and helping to shape it, until the grave opened for the wife, and the children took the old husband back with them to the city.

But since youth their emotions had been strangely tuned toward places they had never seen, and this feeling increased in the last twenty-five years of their marriage, after the children had gone. Flashes from distant cities kept coming and taking up their thoughts.

When the wife was still a girl at home, two of her older brothers had migrated to Minnesota. She remembered the arguments and her father's unwillingness, but when the boys were of age and determined, he could not hold them. One of them operated a large farm there for the rest of his life. The other went cruising around the West; he was in the Klondike gold rush in 1898 and finally settled in California.

Her younger sister who lived nearby had said that if her husband came back from the Civil War she would never want anything more from life. He returned, a veteran of Gettysburg and other battles, got a job driving the stage to Ellsworth and they settled into a new home. Before very long they lost their two babies, within a week, of diphtheria; they felt they must find some different world, and left to take up a homestead claim in Montana.

Letters used to come from Minnesota, Montana, and California, and from younger members of these families who had gone on to Washington and Idaho. But my Grandmother never saw her two brothers and her sister again. Neither did my Grandfather ever see his eight brothers and sisters again after they left the family home.

From his youth, Grandfather remembered agitation about how to keep up the family standards. His great-grandfather had lived in the first log house built in the settlement and had had the pioneer's land allotment. His grandfather, and great-uncles whom he could remember, had been managers, selectmen, surveyors, constables, fence-viewers, hog-reeves, and jurors, useful citizens during the eighteenth century. His vigorous father was still in lumber. Thirty oxen and some horses milled around in the barnyard of the big homestead, but there was no chance for all the boys.

The parents resisted, and delayed the time of leaving, but in the end five went to California, one to the mother's home in Nova Scotia, and two to Minnesota—all in the hard days when travel was by stage and boat, unless the boys went on foot.

The tragedy of those early separations was that they

were almost as final as death. One of Grandfather's sisters, a single woman, who was working as a seamstress in a western city actually disappeared after an epidemic there. There were delays, inexplicable now, in starting the search and no trace of her was ever found.

Women carried a perpetual heaviness of loss because migrants wrote so seldom. Itinerant canvassers who took orders for enlarging daguerreotypes did a thriving business. Nothing else was left of the absent, except to think and talk of them as they were in childhood and youth. Nevertheless, no one was alone in these partings. Neighbors had the same experience. My grandparents' neighbors on the east had twelve children, of whom eleven went away. On the west, the neighbor had only two; the boy migrated and the girl stayed.

Though the stories told to children of the absent always sounded alike and always spoke of worldly success, the elders also always imparted poetry of place. Western prairies were boundless like the sea, California was almost gold-rimmed and always had roses. The four children of my grandparents had already migrated by the 1870's. The first child stayed at home until she was eighteen. Then she served three years as apprentice at fifty cents a week to a dressmaker in the town, so that she might have a trade to fall back on. At twenty-one, she left for the textile mills in Lawrence, Massachusetts. In order to work there she had to be a church member, go to church regularly, and live in an approved boarding-house. She earned $3 a week as a weaver, tending three looms; as she grew skilled she used to be asked to copy difficult weaves.

Working life made her feel happy and liberated. She paid $1.50 a week for board, had many friends and was always busy with spreads, picnics, and recreation. She read library books and took lecture courses; she went to Boston and enjoyed seeing the Old North Church and hearing Oscar Wilde. She bought a silk frock, a Paisley shawl, and a black satin parasol, and various books. When she had "lung-fever" (pneumonia) in the boarding house, she had almost no attention except what her room-mate could give after working hours.

When New England young women operatives were re-placed by male Irish immigrant labor, she returned to her parents. The next year she married a man in the town, came home every week, and was with her parents to the end. As a widow alone at seventy, she migrated again to New York, but left her name carved and ready upon her husband's tombstone for her final return.

The next daughter taught school briefly and at marriage left for the West. Her winter home in California, her summer cottage up in the mountains, her interest in China and her year in Italy were household legend. She "took up" painting in oils, and the snapshots she sent filled a row of scrapbooks. She used to come back for long visits, yearning for blueberry pie and hating the cold. At the end of her life she willed her estate to the University of California.

The son settled in Minneapolis and his parents never saw him again; he died young. They never saw his children, who moved to Colorado.

The youngest daughter went to the Lawrence mills as a spinner but did not like it and soon returned home. She married and settled on a farm near her parents, with a plan for moving to the city when her children should be of high school age. She moved to New Jersey, returning home or sending a child to visit every few years.

When Grandmother was seventy-seven, after she had

survived the migrations of her brothers and sister and of her own children, she was faced with the migration of her grandchildren. She used to write to all of them every week. To the oldest she said, "I shall never see you again," but also "Tell me more about the Colonial cradle you saw in the Museum; it sounds like one we used to have in the family at home." The fragment that follows she wrote to a girl of eight:

———, Maine,
Sunday,
Jan. the 22nd, 1905.

My Dear,
Now I will tell all I know.
Little Marcia and Jim are going to school
in town. Their mother got a horse, bought a
pung for $12.00, takes them down in the morning and
goes after them at night. It is cold. She
wears a sealskin cap.
Grandpa has got 5 pullets and 10 old hens, he
gets lots of eggs.
How do you like the school in Florida? I know
you must be having a nice time where it is warm
and the Butterflys are out. To-day it snows.
The path over the stile is so icy no one can come in.
How I miss your dear little face, but that is all
in the past. I don't expect to see much more of
you if your father buys a home in New Jersey.
Lots of love,
Grandma.

By the later 1890's migration was routine, the rural population changing to urban population. Transportation was easy, the family conclaves and parental opposition were over. Older brothers and sisters or friends had a place to stay and sometimes a job was already waiting. The young bought a ticket for Boston, left on the evening train with a new steamer trunk, a box of fried chicken, and a promise that "It's only until next summer." Mothers still cried when the train pulled out, but they said it was because they would never have their children as children again.

Against the thinning out must be set the fact that youth, waiting for its time to come, seemed contented. Young men called the father "Father" or "Papa," never "the Old Man." The bitter resentment against farm life in Hamlin Garland's *A Son of the Middle Border* did not exist on our small holdings. Possibly because work had always two outlets, the woods and the land, there was more safety in knowing that farm life was not going on forever. The Unknown was always near enough. When youth most needed change, the change would come.

Those who migrated appeared to secure a higher economic status than those who remained. This may be one of the illusions. Every one who stayed had a home, an education, and a kind of freedom. Migrants moved toward better resources of health, education, religion, and travel, but not as surely to more initiative, better housing, or better use of leisure.

Probably migration made for equality of the sexes, since girls as well as boys expected to leave home. Since travel was romance, it may have delayed other romance and made for individualism. There may be a relationship between migration and fertility. Possibly migration, which delays the age of marriage and sets personal achievement or a new life in another location as the goals, makes such demands of the psychic resources that biological fertility lessens.

My own family has records of the family's migrations on both sides for thirteen generations, back to 1630. About one person in every five changed home and background, either as young single folk, bridal couples, or young parents with small children. In our records, the people who did the migrating were not the parents of large families; it was their children, in the first generation after migration, who produced large families.

Grandmother's brother, who went to Minnesota in 1847 had three children; but the daughter who inherited the farm had eleven. The largest family in our recent records was that of a man (1814–1886) with twenty-two children, whose brother and sister living nearby each had nine. The parents all stayed where they were born. The children who lived to maturity all migrated. In only a lifetime's length, not one of the forty children of these three prolific people remained in the area.

It happened the same way in other places. George Woodbury in *John Goffe's Legacy* * tells the history of a homestead on the Merrimac River, three miles below Manchester, New Hampshire, from 1744 to the present. Migration began in 1850, after the colonial settlement of the forest reached its peak. In 1900, the population was only half its highest figure. The place has become large again now, as a residential area for those who work elsewhere. A woodlot on the homestead has recently been sold for houses for 120 families. *Plainville, USA,* ** is about an Ozark village of sixty-five houses and 275 people. In Plainville, one half of each generation migrated. Beginning after the Civil War, all those who could not inherit farms had to go West.

* George Woodbury, *John Goffe's Legacy* (New York: W. W. Norton & Company, Inc., 1950).
** James West, *Plainville, USA* (New York: Columbia University Press, 1945).

The westward movement must have taken the more aggressive personalities out of the community, just as war does. Over the years, the steady departure of the young starved the hamlet of rude strength and the youthful point of view and left the prevailing opinion elderly. Nothing was built; nothing new happened.

When the United States was more rural and sociologists made more studies of rural life, they were concerned with preventing the city from draining the country of the young. The city did drain our hamlet, of course; the earth lay very thinly over the stones there, and the best growth of the woods had already been cut. In earlier times, the very process of exhaustion had an aura of romance and both parents and children knew its bouquet.

13

Fifty Years Afterward

THE NATIVE RETURNING thinks at first:

> No change though you lie under
> The land you used to plow.

This echo is not really true now, the time has been too long. The individual is going or gone, and mournful grass grows on the path that used to lead home. Human change is vast. The place itself stays.

The great change is that the lovely land of isolation now seems connected with the world. The connection begins with the town and the hamlet. They are tied together as they were not at the end of the nineteenth century. The hamlet is a ribbon development, with no strong focus such as a green; this suggests that the town and the hamlet may in time become a single unit, as they were in the beginning.

Change comes first to the eyes. The Gothic treetops still rim the horizon, the salt hay marshes and the curve of the main river lie in the familiar sweep. The scene has not shrunken; it has not even changed in essentials, except that the hamlet has more trees. The tamarack feathers and soars. Forest clearings which used to be cow pastures full of ferny masses and raspberry thickets growing in brush piles are gone to woods again in groves of fir, spruce, and pine.

The waters of Middle River are still blue but engineering, to control the tidal salt water, has diminished its flow. The *Margaretta* could not now be floated up to the basin on a night's tide. Sharp-edged sea grass grows out of muck at the spot where she was anchored. In the hamlet the ocean seems nearer, partly because eight miles is no great distance for an automobile, but also because of the seagulls always flying overhead. The gulls came after a city dump was laid out in the marshes.

The beloved balm-of-Gilead trees and the old willows are gone, but new tree giants have succeeded them. By moonlight they make deep black shadows where no shadows used to be. The hamlet had few elms, but one door-yard stripling of 1900 now stands forty feet high. Some time during the half century the whip-poor-will arrived. He calls his name a thousand times in the summer dusk. The landscape still gives to the sixth sense a warning of cold to come.

The town's looks, too, continue to follow the old pattern remarkably. The street plans made for horse and foot traffic have been well adapted to the automobile. Old trees of stately growth still shade all but Main and Center streets. The homes have held on to both lawns and flowers. The post-war industry, a rayon mill in red brick, has been folded into its site on the river bank so successfully that it would not disgrace the Harvard Yard. The Opera House has burned, but the civic functions of the Opera House have been taken over by the new State Teachers College buildings on the hill.

The population of the area—a shire town, two satellite towns, a village, and the hamlet—is approximately the same as that of fifty years ago. Its peak of population was 6,987 in 1870, its lowest ebb 4,390 in 1930 and 1940; its 1950 count was 6,014, which included the latest United States Census enumeration of 1,621 people in the unincorporated neighborhoods on the outskirts of the town. These neighborhoods were there, under the same names, in the 1900's; transportation now pulls them toward the center. The town and the hamlet—trading and residential places—are almost exactly the size they were in 1900. Population in the hamlet is maintained by new people coming in from further out in the country, balancing the numbers who have migrated. But the two satellite towns and the village have lost almost half their population; they had been lumber and fishing villages and their loss is a consequence of changes in these industries.

The pale dusty road with the remembered hollows has turned dark and smooth and draws everything nearer to the town. It lies exactly as it used to, a winding loop with one branching road, two connecting streets, and farm lanes turning off at the same places. The ghosts of the long past who used to walk the dirt roads do not come to the hard surface. The women in long dresses, the men driving truck carts, the first high-wheeled bicycle, the horse who ran a mile in two minutes are really gone.

The houses are fading too. The old ones are fifty years older and usually without paint, sometimes needing repairs. The United States Census of Housing in 1940 enumerates fifty-one dwellings of which forty-two were owner-occupied, three tenant-occupied, and six vacant. Two houses had bathrooms, thirty-six had toilets in the structure, sixteen had running water, nineteen had electric light, twenty-two houses were in need of major repairs. Average monthly rent at that time was $4.17 in the hamlet and $15.88 in the town. The number of homes is now about the same as in the 1890's. The new homes only balance the loss of the five destroyed by fire, the sites of four of these are obliterated, well-sweeps gone and poplars and cedars growing to twenty-five feet out of the cellar holes. A stand of hemlocks has taken possession of Aunt Hannah's house which burned soon after her death. The three white gravestones of her heart stand straight and the inscriptions are still clear. Raspberries and blueberries grow heavily on her land and wasps zoom in her yard. The apple trees from which she broke blossoming branches for Memorial Day are shrinking, but still bear flower and fruit. The great-grandfather's old homestead for the nine children, all but one of whom migrated, is now a boarding home for old men.

The deterioration of the older houses may be more in looks than in fact. A house which, according to the assessed valuation, might have brought $800 if sold in 1900 was for sale in 1955 at an asking price of $4,000. Houses are still roomy and very likely substantial enough, but from shining white houses with green blinds they have weathered to grey. Paint used to be one of the articles of faith; now only the exceptional older house is painted. However, these houses were built by good craftsmen. Grey and out of repair, they still have beautiful proportions and the look of belonging to the earth. Their bulk on the ground stands solidly and the roof slopes are as satisfying as the curves of cattle.

Recent housing is lower in architectural standards than

that of the nineteenth century and lacks the ancient beauty. The trim small Cape Codders are constructed by rule, without the personal stamp of the builder. They might be in any builder's development anywhere. A few little boxes of shelter have been built by children on the parents' land, by sons about to be married who have ventured on carpentry. Small, unpainted, without a garden setting, these are more like summer places than like the historic homes.

All the households have lost the flowery aura and the dooryard setting. The beds of sweet peas, pansies, phlox, petunias, candytuft, and mignonette were only annuals; they could be removed as easily as the croquet set. Bleeding-heart can be frozen out and even the big rosy weigelas of which women used to be so proud are not perpetual. Grass grows long now and sometimes turns to hay between the road and the door. The large vegetable gardens and the waving corn and potato fields stretching out just beyond the lawns are gone too because people find it easier to buy vegetables.

Those employed at non-farming work prefer to buy milk and butter, so cattle, and the calves tethered in dooryards, have mostly disappeared. There are no sheep, and horses are as rare today as oxen were in the 1890's. An occasional farm has a few horses out to pasture; only the Lumber Company has bunches of blacks and bays in the yard, waiting for winter use.

The new elements about the dooryard are the car and truck. They shine with paint; the time and money that used to go into the upkeep of the house and flowers now go to the car. Cars on the street are still black for the most part, but red, green, and blue ones are edging in and Cadillacs are represented. Improved transportation also accounts for more consciousness of the county, Washington County.

Just as there is more awareness of county and state, so there is more awareness of national and international affairs. Many homes had sons in World War II. The first farm visited in the hamlet had sent four sons and had at that time a grandson flying a jet in Korea. The last home visited had sent four sons and lost one of them on the Normandy beaches.

Even while looking at landscape and houses, the eye sees changes in the appearance of the people. Country folk used to seem set apart, both by their bodies and their clothes, as being of the country. They have lost this distinctness.

The bodies are not gnarled as they used to be by late middle age. The woman does not have to work so hard; she is stouter. The man looks of the same weight and stature as before. He is more twisted than the woman; he still lifts, tugs, and struggles with the law of gravity. He may not be more one-sided than the city man who always carries a heavy briefcase. He struggles less than his father did. He may have access to a power saw instead of sawing his wood by hand. He does not have to haul rocks and fill to repair potholes in the road or shovel his way through snowdrifts out to other men. The snowplow begins to move soon after the storm starts and even if he lives at the end of a long lane the plow breaks through the snow to his door.

Clothes are inconspicuous. Babies playing by the roadside wear the same pink sun suits they would be wearing in the New York suburbs. As the traveler drives back into the woods, fifteen miles from anywhere, the road passes a house in a clearing. The front door opens and a fifteen-year-old girl runs across the yard. She wears blue jeans, a T-shirt, white socks and loafers, and her hair flies out in a pony tail. She has the matching adolescent face too, alive with a rebellion the girl of the last century never would have dared to show. This girl's mother if she chances to come outdoors is certain to have a permanent wave and may wear high-heeled red shoes.

Probably it is a sign of the good life that the newspaper advertises "ladies' dungarees . . . $2.69, crepe nightgowns . . . $1.39, mesh panties . . . $.29." Country clothing used to be anything but "mesh." Now it is gayer in color, lighter in weight, less durable. The originality and eccentricity of frocks made over at home has given way to uniformity, influenced by sport styles.

Hair looks luxuriant and well cared for. On women, it now begins to be curled at eighteen. Every woman used to be her own hairdresser; now the town has three professionals and an appointment is hard to get. Hats are little worn in summer; it used to be considered unhealthy and radical to go bareheaded. A bareheaded woman might bear watching about other unauthorized things.

Teeth used to be a possible source of expensive misfortune after thirty-five. The cost of dentistry was as much dreaded in the late nineteenth century as hospitalization for observation is now. Fairly young women might have sunken lips and a porcelain smile because, at the first serious toothache, they had decided to go to meet the future, taking ether and acquiring false teeth. Men had a more obstinate attitude; they took care of extracting their own teeth, one at a time. In old age, the mouth under the mustache still had a few discolored teeth, not matched for biting. An evidence of improvement in dental care is that teeth are no longer noticeable.

No doubt money is still the problem it was, but now not everyone believes that doing without is better than having because want strengthens the character. Technically, the hamlet has changed from a subsistence economy to a money economy, with discernible interest in spending in the American way. Bottled gas ranges and appliances, refrigerators and television, are advertised. Slab wood already cut for the stove is $5 a truck load at the mill. A Loan Company offers "easy loans, $25 to $300."

Meals are still eaten three times a day, but not necessarily at home. Once, the only food that could be bought abroad was the Fourth of July church dinner in the hamlet and the twenty-five cent church supper in the town. Big spenders went to the Methodist supper one night, the Universalist the next, and the Congregationalist the third.

Eating outside the home is now well established. One of the leading restaurants of the area, two miles out of town, advertises "Turkey Dinner every Sunday . . . $1.00, One Lb. Sirloin Steak Dinner . . . $1.85." The town has three restaurants and two luncheonettes of the drugstore type. One restaurant serves first-class home cooking of the regional food: fish, clams, baked beans, chicken, hot biscuits, strawberries and cream, shortcakes, blueberry pie. Within two miles driving are two more eating places, one specializing in lobster, the other a tearoom with dainty cooking and mountains of frosted cakes. Restaurants are advertising for waitresses and nothing is heard of the "self-indulgence" of eating between meals. The change in eating expenditures shows itself every Saturday noon when cars from neighboring hamlets park in front of the drugstore and disgorge a father, mother, and four children, all of whom go in and have hamburgers, coffee or cokes, and ice-cream. The parents always used to go to town alone and start back in time to reach home for dinner.

The one-time Prohibition state sells liquor in the state

stores, the newspaper advertises wine and ale, and the local Court hands out fines for drunken driving. Smoking is still not a conspicuous habit. Young men do not smoke constantly and women smoke but little.

New ways to travel have quadrupled the zones of communication, shopping, health services, and recreation. A student at college in Boston usually travels by bus. Greyhound tickets to Boston, one way, cost $8.85 in 1953; to New York City, $13.35. Daily bus service runs not only to the west but to the Canadian provinces, once unknown country. The morning and evening trains run at about the same time they began with in 1896.

Getting and sending letters used to be limited to about three times a week; a family went to the post office once a week and sent mail by neighbors once or twice more. Rural free delivery now runs daily. Fifty years ago when a man went by galloping the horse after the doctor, women in the houses he passed would drop everything and start for his home, saying "I wonder what next." Doctors now are at the other end of the telephone. Before the day of arranging visits by telephone, guests took a chance on finding friends at home. If the house were empty and the horse gone, their fifteen mile trip was for nothing.

The horse and buggy shopper bought everything in town, nothing from mail order catalogues. Everyone shopped at the Emporium for drygoods; this shop was not replaced after a fire, and long grass and fireweed grow upon its site. In its place are smaller specialty shops, a five and ten cent store, a gift shop, a drycleaning establishment, the drugstore, and newstand counters. For large purchases, the consumer drives in a day to Eastport, Calais, Lubec and Ellsworth, little cities of 3,000 to 5,000. In the town—not far from the place that took orders, long ago—

for the Thanksgiving celery and the chrysanthemums from Boston—the grocery stores carry any food obtainable in an average New York City grocery and at about the same prices.

People travel even farther for health reasons than they do for shopping. For the dentist, the oculist, and the aurist, for operations and long treatment, they drive the seventy miles to Bangor, the nearest large city which has an old and favorably known hospital. The town has new private ventures in medical care: a hospital run by a doctor, a maternity home, and a nursing home. Formerly, doctors were almost never seen in the hamlet; now only a telephone call and an automobile bring the doctors from town on short notice.

Motoring has also added vacation zones, and indeed, the very concept of vacation. Solid townspeople used to believe in occasional travel as "broadening," but they disapproved of the summer vacation. A man had no need of a vacation, an employee who wanted one was trying to get above himself, a woman's craving for change in scene was charming only before marriage. Nevertheless, even in the 1880's and '90's some young marrieds insisted on having summer homes whether their fathers—at the head of the family business—liked it or not. An exclusive little summer colony grew, Newport fashion, at the ocean. Here houses and grounds were as large as at the winter home, and the scale of living and entertainment was elaborate. Husbands commuted daily or came just for the week-end.

This little Newport still continues, looking just the same; but the grandchildren have become interested in the lakes instead of the ocean. The four lakes within ten miles are now surrounded by cabins and campers. At the same time, occupancy of old family homes just for the summer is increasing. Cottages are also being located down the peninsulas toward the ocean. The *Want Ads* carry listings of cottages for rent or for sale, and in July someone advertised for "the largest piece of land $125 will buy." Summer sports have also become popular in the area, and are indeed an attraction. The Girls' Camp Week of 1953, offering special instruction in archery and swimming, enrolled girls from all over. Sportsmen travel widely looking for primitive fishing and hunting country, and deep sea fishing has become a week-end sport.

The hamlet and the town used to be sharply divided by occupations. Today they appear united in some ways. With the good transportation, place of residence makes no difference to a job. Commuters are willing to drive up to twenty-five miles, and some mills maintain a bus service for employees. When work lies in the town there is already the pattern for a suburb. Under prosperous conditions this area is probably all one labor market.

The occupations of the rural population would no longer be classified as farming with secondary work in the woods. The rayon mill employs 150 people in three shifts, and some of them are from the hamlet. Other men from the hamlet work steadily in the town stores or around cars. The lumber industry, managed by a corporation, goes on, thirty-five miles or more back in the forest. There is even one of the individual operators who is reviving the older custom, a man who came from a nearby hamlet. But local men no longer work in the woods in winter. The present operatives are seasonal migrants from French Canada. Talk is that the Yankee does not begin to work in the woods young enough to get a feeling for it, while the French Canadian begins as soon as he can swing an axe. The woodsman now earns $100 and up per week. Logs are no longer floated down the rivers in spring; they are sawed into lengths in the woods and sent by truck to the railway. The son of the man they used to call a river driver is now more likely to be a truck driver. For young men, truck-driving, said to pay $45 a week, is an important occupation.

Berries have become a major crop. Men never used to pick blueberries; it was women's and children's work. Now men rake them, and a skilled hand can make from $10 to $40 a day. Blueberries are raised in the hamlet by scientific methods with new burns, spraying, prescribed care, and factory marketing. A day's strawberry picking four miles away netted 7,000 baskets in July. Raspberries too are raised as profitable crops.

The work of the women in the culture is easier now. The countrywoman has less to do with milk, butter, and farm animals, less knitting and sewing, rugmaking and quiltmaking. The town woman may have a washing machine. The number of jobs available does not permit many of the married women to work outside the home. Not every woman drives the family car; long ago, there were women who never learned to harness and drive a horse.

These days, the vocational opportunities in the town which are open to high school graduates are available too to the boys and girls of the hamlet who all go by bus to the town high school. The hamlet pays the tuition. In the hamlet itself, the two one-room schools which used to hold sessions for twenty weeks in a year have been combined. Classes meet in the better of the two old buildings. There are two teachers for Grades I through VIII and the school year is thirty-eight weeks long. The elementary school bus stops at every child's door.

The town high school of 1900 made a reputation preparing for entrance to Harvard, Bowdoin, Smith, Wellesley, and Mount Holyoke. College preparation determined the curriculum and those who could not manage Latin and Algebra dropped out. Four years of English and four of Latin were offered, and three each of Greek and Mathematics, two of either French or German, and two of Ancient History. Science, athletics, and extra-curricular activities did not exist. Casual talk in the town is that Latin has fallen, fallen, although a little Latin Club of adults and students reading together held on until recent years. Pupils are unwilling to learn the grammar and vocabulary necessary for the classics. General courses and business courses are popular. Today's course of study is said to be "more democratic, less thorough."

The State Teachers College in the town has a hundred county students. It has Institutes in Education, Foreign Affairs, and the like. College students who do not go to the State Teachers College at home are likely to attend the University of Maine. In this corner of the state, the University figures as a power now, where it barely existed fifty years ago. Its agricultural department experiments with reforestation, and improvement of the blueberry and other crops.

The Public Library in the town has more books, but still only one librarian on duty at a time. Residents of the hamlet may now draw books upon payment of a fee. The weekly newspaper of home news, eight pages, sells for $2 a year. The New York *Times* and the Boston newspapers of the day before and current Portland and Bangor papers are on the newsstands. A Photographer's Studio supplies good pictures and photographic service.

Arts in the town have had a setback in the death of the last survivor of the family which had been the chief music patron for two generations. Both town and country people have radios, but not television. The town movie house was showing the film about the life of Toulouse-Lautrec in July, 1953. The owner shows good pictures in a pleasant interior and her management is praised.

The mother Congregational Church and the churches she helped to found in the vicinity still dominate the landscape. John Marin painted the town church spire twice and Ernest Fiene has shown a painting of the white church within the last few years. But although this part of Maine is historically Congregational, the intellectual quality and the reserve of the denomination do not lend themselves to promotion, and signs of a wish for a more emotional faith may be seen. In a neighboring town a Primitive Baptist Church is drawing a relatively large attendance. If you drive into the county from the north, one of the first large buildings is a Church of Jesus Christ of Latter-Day Saints. In the hamlet, the summer afternoon preaching services have dropped to a six-week period. The community Sunday School began in July, 1953, with thirty-four children.

People say that the church is less influential than it used to be, but this has been said since the time of the first churches. "God sent the colonists liberty, but with it, leanness of soul." Changes in education and religion are praised today because they get to more people and lamented because they take less thought.

Manners as a tourist sees them are considerate and reserved, much as they used to be. Driving manners are easy on the nerves. There is no traffic light and no sense of needing any. Cars wait carefully at side streets and drivers offer courtesies to strangers.

The "aristocracy" in both town and hamlet looks somewhat outnumbered by younger sets whose social ties are horizontal, depending on similarities of income and jobs, rather than vertical, depending on family and exclusiveness. This does not exactly mean the absence of social stratification but a transition in its form.

Looking around from any hilltop, seeing no other car for long intervals, fancy wanted the illusion that the familiar houses in their accustomed places still held the familiar people of long ago. In about eight of the fifty-one homes, the longing came true, At least one family who lived there in the years 1894–1904 survived, at ages ranging from sixty-five to over ninety. One woman who had migrated to Nova Scotia was still living at 102. In seven more households, children or grandchildren were the owners.

In ways beyond Lazarus, these fifteen homes show the miracle of continuing life. Someone in the grave for years reappears again in a grandchild's body or a middle-aged daughter's face. A man born in 1845 stood looking at me out of his son's body with his son's eyes. The eyes were liquid, brown, feral, and wary, the body still turned with quick impulse; the organism lingered on from Daniel Boone's day. This man, and the father he represented, had been hunter and woodsman. In old age his recurrent memories were all of thick forest on the unnamed Plantations to the north. He had built log cabins there and he could not remember a winter, before his hunting activities were stopped by the doctor, when he had not gotten a deer. One woman long gone has left a daughter in replica. The golden hair grows again exactly; the height, the figure, the fair skin, the blue eyes, even the smile are hers.

The effect of migration in the hamlet may be seen by

tracing the thirty children who went to the school in the lower district in the 1890's. Two of the thirty children are lost; they moved away years ago. Twenty-three of the remaining twenty-eight moved to Maine cities or Massachusetts or New York, three moved into the town, two stayed in the hamlet. Twelve of them are now dead; five died before reaching the age of marriage. Of those living to maturity, all but one are married and an average marriage is estimated to have at least two children.

Whether these pupils had more schooling or not, as adults all have been able to make their way in various occupations. Two are college graduates. Of the twelve whose work is known, ten are still working. Five women are housewives, one is a housekeeper taking care of an invalid, another a saleswoman, another an executive. The men include a farmer, a barber, a Superintendent of Roads, and a retired General of the United States Army. One man is said to have changed his social status and became very prosperous.

Whittier could still have written about the site of the old schoolhouse. It remains beautiful, evocative, with the full valley view and the far horizons; it is so isolated now that in winter, twelve deer at a time have been seen nibbling at the neighboring apple trees. The northern pasture, where laurel bloomed and the pond was so good for skating or for watching frogs, has been taken over by the forest. The granite ledges, which used to be palaces or homes or the Andes or whatever was needed in play are lost to sight; the pines cover them. The great trees where the children rested in the shade are gone. The schoolhouse itself has been moved elsewhere; a man took it to a dooryard for a dwelling-house.

If it were near to jobs and transportation, this country-

side would be fought for as residential property; one of
the land grants from the Crown has today only sixteen
houses upon it, four built since 1900. But what is increasing is the trees: second and third growth timber covers the
broad hilly spaces.

When the children of fifty years ago were developing
their style of life, the landscape, which stood for personal
identity, held some baffling structure of fulfillment. Memorable gifts of life came from just living in it. The landscape remains and it can still bless. Since, however, most
people leave, the lover of this place must think of what
the traveler takes away.

When Kipling settled finally in rural England, he saw as
the epitome of his area, a man who worked at building
hedges, Hobden the Hedger; thirty generations of his
family had lived on one spot. Later the poet said, of Cecil
Rhodes whom he saw as the symbol of South Africa:

> Living he was the land and dead,
> His soul shall be her soul.

It may be that Americans can no longer live anywhere
long enough to become the incarnations of places. Motility
makes for hospitality to the little incarnations whereby
every place becomes part of the person. But still the native
place always travels along wherever her children go. And
so the hamlet's glimmering landscape and austere code go
on for a little—one generation—in the new places of their
scattering. Whether or not the pattern of migration
changes, landscape and code well up from memory and
the nervous system to modify urban life. They make for
Suburbia and Exurbia. They are the standard of beauty
and ethics by which the prairie and the Grand Canyon, the

statesman and the teacher, are eventually judged. The migrant is buffeted by new surroundings, is subtly changed; but at his center of life something keeps on being the hamlet. "Living he was the land."